BLACK MADONNA

BLACK MADONNA

A Womanist Look at Mary of Nazareth

Courtney Hall Lee

CASCADE *Books* · Eugene, Oregon

BLACK MADONNA
A Womanist Look at Mary of Nazareth

Cascade Books
An Imprint of Wipf and Stock Publishers
199 W. 8th Ave., Suite 3
Eugene, OR 97401

www.wipfandstock.com

PAPERBACK ISBN: 978-1-4982-9379-2
HARDCOVER ISBN: 978-1-4982-9381-5
EBOOK ISBN: 978-1-4982-9380-8

Cataloguing-in-Publication data:

Lee, Courtney Hall

Black Madonna : a womanist look at Mary of Nazareth / Courtney Hall Lee.

Eugene, OR: Pickwick Publications, 2017 | Includes bibliographical references and index.

Identifiers: ISBN 978-1-4982-9379-2 (paperback) | ISBN 978-1-4982-9381-5 (hardcover) | ISBN 978-1-4982-9380-8 (ebook)

Subjects: LCSH: Mary, Blessed Virgin, Saint | Womanist theology

Classification: BT602 .L315 2017 (paperback) | BT602 (ebook)

Manufactured in the U.S.A.   09/15/17

This book is dedicated to my mother, Shirley, my daughter, Lauren, all of our foremothers, and all of our kinswomen yet to come.

CONTENTS

ACKNOWLEDGMENTS

As I write this on Christmas Eve, I feel especially blessed to have given birth to this project which was conceived in my mind long ago. The opportunity to write this book was an unexpected gift. I thank Wipf and Stock for their support in bringing this title to fruition and their commitment to publishing newcomers and diverse voices.

I would not have found the words or the knowledge to write this volume without the teaching I received from the stellar faculty at Hartford Seminary. I would like to give special thanks to Dr. Najib Awad for his unparalleled example as a dedicated scholar and theologian with a voracious appetite for knowledge and academic excellence. I would not have had the courage to take on this project without the strong foundation his teaching provided. I also give special thanks to Dr. Shanell Smith, whose innovative ideas and approach to her work will propel womanist religious disciplines into the next generation. I am greatly appreciative of Hartford Seminary for providing me with a setting for theological study and research which encourages free thinking, ecumenism, plurality, and community.

I would like to thank my daughter, Lauren, for her understanding and patience with my many hours spent in front of the keyboard, and for inspiring me to use my voice in ways that I hope will make a difference in her world. I thank my faithful toy poodle, Foxy, for sitting at my feet from my first keystrokes to my final product. Finally, I thank my husband, Eric, for his constant support, intellectual engagement, and encouragement, which allows me to do this work that I love.

INTRODUCTION

Ain't I a Mother?

Each year, the seasons of Advent and Christmas pass by, and along with them one of the only times we Protestants talk about Mary. We all love the familiar and comforting narrative: Mary about to give birth, a journey following a mystical star, a couple taking shelter in a lowly, but comfortable manger. And a young, virtuous girl, most highly favored, bearing the world a savior. Once she has the baby, the kings come for the epiphany and we do not hear from Mary again until next year.

My family and I once moved away from an affluent Connecticut suburb to the City of Hartford. The neighborhood was equal parts Mark Twain Victorian and twenty-first-century urban. The color of city life surrounded us. As a result of the move, my daughter entered second grade at a nearby Catholic school. One afternoon, a few weeks into the school year, I found my daughter with one of my scarves draped over her head. She chose one that was a light, airy, robin's-egg blue. She looked at me and squealed, "I'm Mary!" It was then that realized that I was getting an ecumenical education at home.

Honoring Mary gives most Protestants the heebie-jeebies. For those of us who were raised with a Reformed theology, what we were taught of Catholics was that they were gravely misguided because of their prayers to Mary and the saints. I once heard an evangelical minister speak of a person being "delivered from the cult of Catholicism," citing Marian veneration as one of the faith's false teachings. While I did not have a full understanding of the concept of intercessory prayer or Mary's role in it, I agreed with what I had been taught without much consideration.

As a result of our collective heebie-jeebies, the Protestant conversation about Mary has been limited to only two main points: she bore Jesus in a manger and she saw Jesus after his resurrection. In our defense, there isn't that much more of her in the Gospels. Without Catholic or Orthodox tradition, what role should Mary play, if she is to have any role at all?

The first time I spent much time thinking about Mary was the Advent season during my pregnancy. My husband and I were invited to light the pink joy candle. The two of us, a couple in a season of waiting for our own baby to be born. The expectation that Mary must have felt resonated with me as I experienced pregnancy. I also realized for the first time how afraid she must have been. A first pregnancy is scary, physically and emotionally. A great responsibility has been given, and we have no real idea what it will be like until it happens. If I was afraid during my completely unremarkable pregnancy, what must Mary have been going through? Unmarried, betrothed to a man, and impregnated by the Holy Spirit. That is a lot to handle.

During my pregnancy, I had an experience that allowed me to relate to Mary's position as an unmarried mother-to-be in a society with staunchly patriarchal mores. I was standing in line at a local coffee shop. I remember that I was wearing a red T-shirt and capri pants. I had one of those little drawstring backpacks slung onto my back, a style that was popular with teens at the time.

In front of me was a sizable group of Black girls from the nearby public high school, buying after-school treats. In back of me was a middle-aged white woman. I momentarily turned to the side, revealing my rounded profile. The woman behind me noticed my large belly, and I heard her "tsk" in disgust and let out an audible, "Oh my God."

I stiffened up as I realized that she thought I was a part of the group of high school girls. She saw a young, Black, unwed mother, not even out of high school. In actuality I was twenty-seven years old, happily married, an Ivy League grad, and a young lawyer. But she didn't know that. She just saw a pregnant girl who should not be pregnant. Someone lowly. A moment later I turned around to look directly at her. It was a woman from my church. The very church where I lit that joy candle a few months earlier. That moment was my first taste of Black motherhood.

Black motherhood has always been loaded and laden with stereotypes, hardships, and sacrifices. During the time of American slavery, Black children could be bought, sold, beaten, and raped as property. The realities of mothering during slavery were unbearable. For many years after the end of slavery, Black women were relegated as subservient to white women as domestic workers, all the while raising their white children. In the twenty-first century, Black mothers live in fear of state-sanctioned, racially motivated violence. The stories of seventeen-year-old Trayvon Martin and twelve-year-old Tamir Rice are etched in our brains. Black American motherhood is deeply complex. At times it is just plain painful.

The Christian faith has been a source of sustenance for Black women for centuries. This has always seemed illogical to many, as Christianity was the religion of our captors. However, Black women have been able to take ownership over Christianity, forming their own theology of liberation. They do this by forming a tight bond with Jesus Christ.

Black women have valued the figure of Christ since the time of slavery. Jesus provides comfort in two ways. First, by viewing his suffering on the cross as analogous to their own suffering. For Black women, Christianity has provided a place where they could empathize with the violent and undeserved plight of Jesus on the cross. Second, by his triumph over death and his promise of everlasting life, Jesus promises something better once we come into God's kingdom. Belief in Christ provides an afterlife that promises redemption and restitution, in the form of the Father's many mansions.

The Black church has always been anchored by women.[1] Though some Black churches still keep women out of the pulpit, the matriarchs known as "church mothers" are the unofficial council of elders who are the heart of the church. If you show up in the sanctuary of a predominantly Black Sunday service, you will find more women than men.

While Black women over the ages have faithfully called on Jesus, Mary has been virtually invisible in the Black religious experience. Black Americans are overwhelmingly Protestant. Baptist, Pentecostal, and evangelical theologies dominate the institution known as the Black church. Black women certainly have a womanist take on Christology, as detailed in Jacquelyn Grant's book *White Women's Christ, Black Women's Jesus*. But any relationship between Black women and Mother Mary has been nearly nonexistent.

The motherhood experience has defined Black women since they set foot on American soil. Because slavery treated Blacks as chattel, Black women were treated as breeding stock. Black women were also subject to sexual dominion by their white masters, resulting in countless children

---

1. I refer to the Black Church as the historical institution of African-American Christianity which exists today in predominantly Black congregations.

who were the product of rape. Their wombs were not their own. Once they did bear children, they birthed them into an abject life of slavery. They also lived with the weight of knowing that family members could be sold away forever.

Between the Black esteem for Jesus and the degradation of Black mothers, it would seem that Mary would be a natural ally for Black women. After all, she bore the world a savior. Her role was to carry a baby in a frightful situation, and that baby was the Son of God. Finally, she watched as her son was crucified, buried, and rose from the dead. There must be something that Black women can gain from Mary.

In Part 1 of this book, I examine Black motherhood, carefully considering the effects of slavery, social inferiority through domestic work and Jim Crow, and pervasive societal stereotypes of Black women. In Part 2, I provide an overview of traditional Mariology, presenting the history of Marian doctrine in the Eurocentric church as well as Islam. Next, I examine the intersection between Christology and traditional Mariology. Finally, I consider the existing feminist critique of Marian doctrine.

In the third and final part of this book, I lay the framework for the concept of a womanist Mariology. This begins with a look at postmodern Black motherhood, focusing contextually on racially motivated gun violence by police officers and vigilantes against Black children. Next I give an overview of the current state of womanist theology and biblical interpretation. I argue that the true first wave of womanist theology and hermeneutics predates the entry of Black women into the academy, taking a look at the religious aspects of slave narratives. I then give a brief summary of the work of several womanist thinkers in the second and third waves of womanist scholarship. The next chapters take on the challenging juxtaposition of Mary's virginity with the history of sexual exploitation Black women, and a view of the *Magnificat* through the lens of liberation theology. Finally, I conclude through arriving at a womanist Mariology, honoring a womanist version of Mary as Black Madonna, which gives a new concept of Marian veneration through a womanist scope.

As a Black, Protestant woman, I have always been taught to be a daughter of old, faithful Sarah, and an admirer of the loyal and resourceful Ruth. The "Proverbs 31 woman" has long been held as the gold standard for women. Now, it is time for Mary to have her place in the sun. Let's get to intimately know the mother of our Jesus Christ. After all, no one is as important in the Black family as a mother.

PART 1

BLACK MOTHERHOOD: A HISTORY

1

MOTHERHOOD DURING AMERICAN SLAVERY

The atrocity of human trafficking from Africa led to millions of Black people living in slavery. From the time that African people were captured, their lives were stripped of dignity and their existing family units were irreparably broken. Black women's autonomy was stolen from the first moments of European contact, as their heads were shaved out of sanitation purposes for the hellish journey through the Middle Passage.

In the institution of chattel slavery, Blacks were considered property, not people. Because of this, enslaved people had no right to have a family. Opportunities for marriage or committed relationships were not guaranteed, and opportunities for partnerships were limited.[1] However, as the profitability of owning slaves increased over time, slave owners began to encourage Black marriage as a stable source of new slaves. Black people were now a renewable resource through breeding, and some believed that marriage would help keep slaves complacent.[2] Because of chattel slavery, Black motherhood in America became a commodity that would produce a free labor source for generations. Enslaved women were referred to with the demeaning term "brood-sows" and were treated as such.[3]

Black motherhood was harrowing from the time women first gave birth. Black infants were usually born with low birth weights. They were

1. Hallam, "Slave Experience: Family," page 1, lines 8–11.

2. Ibid., page 1, lines 68–71.

3. Jones, *Labor of Love*, 9–10.

3

forced to wean early so that their mothers could work again as soon as possible. Because of this, Black babies lacked the vital nutrition provided by breast milk and ate a meager diet of gruel, cornbread, vegetable soups, or whatever soft food was available. This diet lacked sorely in protein and nutrients. As a result, children born into slavery were very small and malnourished.[4] With this difficult start in life, infant mortality was very high.[5]

Black children were slaves from birth. Children were given simple chores from the time they were small.[6] They began to work in the fields with adults anywhere between ages eight and twelve. Because of their poor health and severe working conditions, the child mortality rate was also very high.[7] Writer Jacqueline Jones writes:

> Parents could hardly voice their objections when their children began their initiation into the arduous world of grown-up labor, and at times mothers and fathers acquiesced willingly because masters increased accordingly the food allotments of youngsters now forced to work hard. And so Black girls and boys followed the mistress's directions in filling wood boxes with kindling, lighting fires in chilly bedrooms . . . making beds, washing and ironing clothes, parching coffee, polishing shoes . . . Mistresses entrusted to the care of those who were little more than babies themselves the bathing, diapering, dressing, grooming and entertaining of white infants.[8]

The harsh life Black mothers and their children faced pushed against every maternal instinct. Black women were not free to nurse their babies as they wished. As a consequence, mothers watched their children's malnourishment worsen. Slave children were punished severely, much like adults.[9] Mothers were powerless to save their children from savage abuse. Slavery robbed children of a healthy childhood, and likewise, deprived Black women of a healthy mothering experience.

The lack of family unit also caused a significant amount of stress on Black families. Most children grew up without fathers. Black fathers were

---

4. Mintz, "Childhood and Transatlantic Slavery," page 1, lines 12–15, 31–35.
5. Ibid.
6. Jones, *Labor of Love*, 19–20.
7. Ibid., 33–34. See also Mintz, "Childhood and Transatlantic Slavery," lines 39–40.
8. Jones, *Labor of Love*, 22.
9. Mintz, "Childhood and Transatlantic Slavery," line 44.

often working and living on a different plantation, making them unavailable to be supportive fathers and husbands.

Some slave children had white fathers as a result of the sexual exploitation of their mothers. These children lived in a twisted world where a slave owner would enslave his own children. As a result, mixed-race children and their mothers faced many difficult family complexities.

The legacy of the mixed-race heritage of Black Americans remains in place today. Activist and former NAACP Chairman Julian Bond spoke of his grandfather, who was fathered by a white slave owner. "My grandfather and his mother were property, like a horse or a chair," Bond said in a speech given at the Lincoln Memorial. "As a young girl she'd been given away as a wedding present to a new bride. And when that bride became pregnant, her husband—that's my great grandmother's owner and master—exercised his right to take his wife's slave as his mistress. That union produced two children, one of them my grandfather."[10]

Black family members were often sold away from each other. Boys were most often sold away because they were stronger workers and therefore more profitable. Girls, however, could also be sold away from their mothers with the knowledge that they would likely be sexually abused by owners or sold into prostitution.[11] Black mothers lived with the constant knowledge that their children could be sold to far off lands, or that they themselves could be sold away from their children. This instability made Black motherhood one long crisis experience.

The pains of motherhood during slavery are well illustrated in *The Narrative of Sojourner Truth*. Truth was born into slavery with the name Isabella. The biographical narrative she dictated to abolitionist author Harriet Beecher Stowe described specific examples of the pain that Black mothers endured during slavery. During her childhood, Sojourner recalled the lifelong anguish that her mother felt because of her separation from all of her children.

> ... she wishes that all who would fain believe that slave parent have not natural affection for their offspring could have listed as *she* did, while Bomefree and Mau-mau Bett,—their dark cellar lighted by a blazing pine-knot,—would sit for hours, recalling and recounting every endearing, as well as harrowing circumstance that taxed memory could supply, from the histories of those dear departed

10. Malloy, "Julian Bond Family Slave History," lines 4, 6–8.
11. Hallam, "Slave Experience: Family," page 2, lines 30–32.

ones, of whom they had been robbed, and for whom their hearts still bled. Among the rest, they would relate how the little boy, on the last morning he was with them, arose with the birds, kindled a fire, calling for his Mau-mau to "come, for all was now ready for her"—little dreaming of the dreadful separation which was so near at hand . . .[12]

Sojourner eventually experienced her own pains of motherhood. She spoke of raising her children to survive in their harsh environment. She recalls watching her children suffer from hunger rather than risk stealing from the master's family: "The Lord only knows how many times I let my children go hungry, rather than take secretly the bread I liked not to ask for."[13]

The narrative goes on to detail Sojourner's experiences with physical abuse: "When he had tied her hands together before her, he gave her the most cruel whipping she was ever tortured with. He whipped her till the flesh was deeply lacerated, and the blood streamed from her wounds."[14] Sojourner also endured sexual abuses at the hands of both her master and mistress.[15]

The accounts of Black motherhood during slavery illustrated in Sojourner Truth's narrative give us a glimpse into the life of one particular Black woman during slavery. Countless others's stories go untold. We can only imagine these women and their untold plights.

Black Wet Nurses and Caregivers

Another wedge between Black mothers and their children was the fact that Black women were often forced to breastfeed and care for white children at the expense of their own. Black mothers who had recently given birth were often required to wean their infants and nurse a White one. At times, however, the Black mother would nurse both her own child and the master's child simultaneously.[16]

Black women were also engaged in the house as "mammies." A mammy was a Black woman who worked in the owner's household, doing

12. Truth and Perry, *Narrative of Sojourner Truth*, 11.

13. Ibid., 27.

14. Ibid., 19.

15. Ibid., 21.

16. Parkhurst, "Role of the Black Mammy," 358.

housework but mainly caring for their mistress's children. "Mammy" cared for the master's children entirely, including feeding, dressing, bathing, and every aspect of care usually given by a mother.[17]

The image of the mammy has been highly romanticized in white culture. This mythical figure—fat, jolly, wise and beloved—is a well-known construct that is entirely rooted in fiction. Black feminist scholar Patricia Hill Collins points out that the life expectancy of an enslaved woman was 33.6 years.[18] If this is the case, slave women likely died much too young to fit the stereotypical mammy description. It is more likely that a mammy was a frail young girl or woman who had recently given birth to her own children, charged with the exhausting work of motherhood on someone else's behalf.

Like Collins, other scholars have challenged the notion for the stereotypical mammy. In her book *Sister Citizen*, journalist Melissa Harris-Perry argues that the image of a happy, content, and grandmotherly mammy is historically inaccurate. Harris-Perry claims that this portrait was created to support white supremacy. By implying that these mammies were jovial and cared for, the institution of slavery is belittled and unrecognized for the human rights abuse that it was.

Gender roles were widely disregarded by slave owners. Women were forced to work in the fields as "human hoeing machines," yet they were also used as "breeders" to produce new slaves.[19] Owners attempted to balance women's role as breeders with their desire to force women to work relentlessly in the fields; a baby in the womb was worth money in the future, but so was every bushel of cotton a woman picked. Thus, an owner's wish to protect a fetus as a resource was often in conflict with their desire to mistreat and overwork its mother. To illustrate this disturbing dichotomy, Jones writes of the ways in which owners physically punished pregnant women while taking care not to kill the fetus:

> The whipping of pregnant and nursing mothers—"so that blood and milk flew mingled from their breasts"—revealed the myriad impulses that conjoined to make women especially susceptible to physical abuse . . . "They were made to lie face down in a specially

---

17. Ibid., 359.
18. Jones, *Labor of Love*, 17.
19. Ibid.

dug depression in the ground," a practice that provided simultaneously for the protection of the fetus and the abuse of its mother.[20]

While slave owners ignored gender norms, Black women usually fulfilled traditional roles at home as wife or mother. After working long days
for the master, they attempted to provide a normal home life by doing the
cooking, cleaning, and making clothes. Enslaved women wanted to provide
as comfortable a household as possible for their families, and felt a sense
of loss if they were kept from doing so. "Dey done it 'cause dey wanted to.
Dey wuz workin' for deyselves den."[21] This round-the-clock responsibility
was the inception of generations of Black women's battle with role strain.

Black motherhood in the United States began a legacy of suffering that
would attach itself to Black motherhood well beyond the end of slavery. After the Emancipation Proclamation, life for many Black Americans did not
change very much. In the next chapter, we will examine the continuation
of Black women's work serving white people in the years beyond slavery.

20. Ibid., 18–19.
21. Ibid., 26.

2

STILL SERVING
Domestic Work Post-Slavery

The American Civil War ended on May 9, 1865. That December, the Thirteenth Amendment was ratified, creating a population of African-American citizens with a free but uncertain future. The sad reality for many Blacks was a life of work that was not very different than slavery. For Black women, many still worked in harsh domestic positions for paltry wages. The age of the mammy continued.

My grandmother, Vivian Howard, was born in 1912, in a rural West Virginia coal town called Winona. She was the ninth child of John and Margaret Howard. Her father was born before the end of the Civil War, during the age of slavery. Vivian was a first-generation freewoman, and her life reflected that social position.

For a young Black woman, Vivian was well educated. She had an eighth-grade education, beautiful penmanship, and strong math skills. In the future, she would fill out income tax forms for her neighbors in the housing projects for three dollars pay. Her intellect, however, did not allow her to overcome her background as a poor Black woman. As a result, she spent many years working as a domestic, doing laundry and housekeeping work.

My grandmother and countless other Black women worked in difficult situations. From the end of slavery well into the twentieth century, Black women continued to perform manual labor, dirty work, and child-rearing for white families. All the while, Black children were left to fend for themselves while their mothers worked to support them.

In a New York City magazine called *The Independent*, a woman described her life as a domestic in a 1912 piece known as "More Slavery at the South," by "a Negro nurse."[1] Her narrative gives us keen insight and a wealth of knowledge about working and living as a Black domestic worker. She speaks candidly about her absence from her own children's lives, the unjust pay rate, and the humiliation of living in the Jim Crow South. She begins with a summary of her work history:

> For more than thirty years—or since I was ten years old—I have been a servant in one capacity or another in white families in a thriving Southern city, which has at present a population of more than 50,000. In my early years I was at first what might be called a "house-girl" . . . Still later I was graduated into a cook, in which position I served at different times for nearly eight years in all. During the last ten years I have been a nurse. I have worked for only four different families during all these thirty years . . . I have been able to become intimately acquainted not only with the lives of hundreds of household servants, but also with the lives of their employers. I can, therefore, speak with authority on the so-called servant question; and what I say is said out of an experience which covers many years.[2]

She then speaks of the working conditions of the greater Black community, demonstrating the way that work situations had not changed much since the abolishment of slavery:

> To begin with, then, I should say that more than two-thirds of the negroes of the town where I live are menial servants of one kind or another . . . nurses, cooks, washerwomen, chambermaids, seamstresses, hucksters, janitresses, and the like. I will say, also, that the condition of this vast host of poor colored people is just as bad as, if not worse than, it was during the days of slavery. Tho today we are enjoying a nominal freedom, we are literally slaves.[3]

The woman then substantiates these claims by providing a detailed account of what her work days entail. The hours and demands were grueling and unreasonable, with no labor rights or regard for personal life:

1. "More Slavery at the South."
2. Ibid., lines 2–11.
3. Ibid., lines 12–16.

I frequently work from fourteen to sixteen hours a day. I am compelled to by my contract, which is oral only, to sleep in the house. I am allowed to go home to my own children, the oldest of whom is a girl of 18 years, only once in two weeks, every other Sunday afternoon—even then I'm not permitted to stay all night. I not only have to nurse a little white child, now eleven months old, but I have to act as playmate, or "handy-andy," not to say governess, to three other children in the house, the oldest of whom is only nine years of age. I wash and dress the baby two or three times each day; I give it its meals, mainly from a bottle; I have to put it to bed each night; and, in addition, I have to get up and attend to its every call between midnight and morning. If the baby falls to sleep during the day, as it has been trained to do every day about eleven o'clock, I am not permitted to rest. It's "Mammy, do this," or "Mammy, do that," or "Mammy, do the other," from my mistress, all the time. So it is not strange to see "Mammy" watering the lawn with the garden hose, sweeping the sidewalk, mopping the porch and halls, mopping the porch and halls, helping the cook, or darning stockings. Not only so, but I have to put the other three children to bed each night as well as the baby, and I have to wash them and dress them each morning. I don't know what it is to go to church; I don't know what it is to go to a lecture or entertainment of anything of the kind; I live a treadmill life; and I see my own children only when they happen to see me on the streets when I am out with the children, or when my children come to the "yard" to see me, which isn't often, because my white folks don't like to see their servants' children hanging around their premises. You might as well say that I'm on duty all the time—from sunrise to sunrise, every day in the week. I am the slave, body and soul, of this family. And what do I get for this work—this lifetime bondage? The pitiful sum of ten dollars a month! And what am I expected to do with these ten dollars? With this money I'm expected to pay my house rent, which is four dollars per month, for a little house of two rooms, just big enough to turn around in; and I'm expected, also, to feed and clothe myself and three children.[4]

Unsurprisingly, the nurse includes details of sexual exploitation on the job at the hands of white employers. Though these women were not legally owned as the property of these white men, they still lacked the agency to reject unwanted advances without serious repercussions. Because they needed their jobs for survival and because Black husbands could not hold

4. Ibid., lines 18–35.

white men accountable for these assaults, little difference existed between sexual exploitation during slavery and this era of domestic work.

> Perhaps some might say, if the poor pay is the only thing about which we have to complain, then the slavery in which we daily toil and struggle is not so bad after all. But the poor pay isn't all— not by any means! I remember very well the first and last place from which I was dismissed. I lost my place because I refused to let the madam's husband kiss me. He must have been accustomed to undue familiarity with his servants, or else he took it as a matter of course, because without any love-making at all, soon after I was installed as cook, he walked up to me, threw his arms around me, and was in the act of kissing me, when I demanded to know what he meant, and shoved him away. I was young then, and newly married, and didn't know then that what has been a burden to my mind and heart ever since: that a colored woman's virtue in this part of the country has no protection. I at once went home, and told my husband about it. When my husband went to the man who had insulted me, the man cursed him, and slapped him, and—had him arrested . . . The old judge looked up and said: "This court will never take the word of a nigger against the word of a white man." Many and many a time since I have heard similar stories repeated again and again by my friends. I believe nearly all white men take, and expect to take, undue liberties with their colored female servants—not only the fathers, but in many cases the sons also.[5]

White women were also complicit in the sexual abuse of Black women. The nurse explains the reason white women encouraged or ignored their husbands' egregious behavior.

> I know of more than one colored woman who was openly importuned by white women to become the mistresses of their white husbands, on the ground that they, the white wives, were afraid that, if their husbands did not associate with colored women, they would certainly do so with outside white women, and the white wives, for reasons which ought to be perfectly obvious, preferred to have their husbands do wrong with colored women . . . the fathers of the new generation of Negroes are white men, while their mothers are unmarried, colored women.[6]

5. Ibid., lines 61–73.
6. Ibid., lines 75–80.

As was the case during slavery, Black mothers knew that from a young age their daughters would be subjected to the same sexual exploitation that they experienced:

> I have already told you that my youngest girl was a nurse . . . The very first week that she started out on her work she was insulted by a white man, and many times since has been improperly approached by other white men. It is a favorite practice of young white sports about town—and they are not always young, either—to stop some colored nurse, inquire the name of the "sweet little baby," talk baby talk to the child, fondle it, kiss it, make love to it, etc., etc., and in nine of ten cases every such white man will wind up by making love to the colored nurse and seeking an appointment with her.[7]

The woman giving the narrative was over the age of forty and highly experienced at her job. Still, she was treated with disrespect even by the youngest of white children, showing how deeply racial stratification ran in the postbellum South.

> Another thing—it's a small indignity, it may be, but an indignity just the same. No white person, not even the little children just learning to talk . . . ever thinks of addressing any negro man or woman as Mr., or Mrs., or Miss. The women are called, "Cook," or "Nurse," or "Mammy" . . . In many cases our white employers refer to us, and in our presence, too, as their "niggers."[8]

With this type of deplorable speech, unjustly low pay, and unwanted sexual advances, the Black domestics of the post-slavery South constituted a generation of women who lived exhausting lives.

From my grandmother, Vivian, to the "Negro nurse" who gave us this compelling narrative of the life of an early-twentieth-century domestic, it is clear that the abuses that Black women endured during slavery did not end when Abraham Lincoln signed the Emancipation Proclamation. The very same problems that plagued mothers during slavery continued for generations. As we learned from the insightful Negro nurse, Black children continued to suffer forced neglect, as women were obligated to live with the families of their oppressors instead of their own. They continued to worry for the well-being of their children, who were also exposed to the

7. Ibid., lines 130–36.
8. Ibid., lines 88–92.

general dangers of being Black in their society. For Black women, the cycle individual and societal of abuses did not have an end in sight.

In her conclusion, the eye-opening narrative given by our nurse leaves us with this:

> Perhaps a million of us are introduced daily to the privacy of a million chambers thruout the South, and hold in our arms a million white children, thousands of whom, as infants, are suckled at our breasts—during my lifetime I myself have served as "wet nurse" to more than a dozen white children. On the one hand, we are assailed by white men, and, on the other hand, we are assailed by black men, who should be our natural protectors; and, whether in the cook kitchen, at the washtub, over the sewing machine, behind the baby carriage, or at the ironing board, we are but little more than pack horses, beasts of burden, slaves![9]

> In the distant future, it may be, centuries and centuries hence, a monument of brass or stone will be erected to the Old Black Mammies of the South, but what we need is present help, present sympathy, better wages, better hours, more protections, and a chance to breathe for once while alive as free women.[10]

Black American women have had complex experiences full of pain and indignity. Jim Crow–era domestic work took their ability to nurture their children. This began a cycle of damage to the Black family unit that continues to this day. Black motherhood, however, is not the only identity that Black women carry. Other aspects of Black womanhood, including feminine image, standards of beauty, and sexuality, have also shaped the Black female experience. With these particularized experiences come negative stereotypes. The legacy of "mammy" endures and is a burdening stereotype yoked around the necks of Black women. The next chapter will consider mammy and the other invidious stereotypes attached to Black womanhood.

9. Ibid., lines 142–47.
10. Ibid., lines 147–49.

3

SAPPHIRE, MAMMY, AND JEZEBEL

Stereotypes of Black Women

As examined in the previous chapters, the history of Black women in the United States is fraught with suffering and particularized oppression. Because of this, proper context is crucial to the study of Black women's experiences. The oppressive circumstances under which the Black female image has developed leads to several consistent stereotypes: the Mammy, the Sapphire, and the Jezebel. These harmful stereotypes pervade in the relationship between Black women and society and must be considered in the study of Black women in any discipline.

The Mammy, Sapphire, and Jezebel stereotypes are largely based on depictions of Black women in entertainment and media. In fact, the use of these stereotypes is so prevalent that many people—Black women and others—do not separate them from their opinions of actual Black women. These three basic archetypes have been tightly woven into popular narratives and show up as subtle modern variations like the Welfare Queen, the Video Vixen, or the Angry Black Woman.

In her book *The Sisters Are Alright: Changing the Broken Narrative of Black Women in America*, Tamara Winfrey Harris considers the ways in which these stereotypes affect the way modern Americans relate to Black women, and the way modern Black women relate to themselves. Her poetic preface encapsulates the ways in which Black women have come to embody, embrace and defy these stereotypes.

> I love black women.
> I love the Baptist church mothers in white.
> I love the YouTube twerkers.
> I love the sisters with Ivy League degrees and the ones with GEDs.
> I love the big mamas, ma'dears and aunties.
> I love the loc-wearing sisters who smell like shea butter.
> I love the ladies of the "Divine Nine."
> I love the "bad bitches" in designer pumps and premium lace fronts.
> I love the girls who jumped double Dutch and played hopscotch.
> I love the Nam-myoho-renge-kyo chanters, the seekers and the athiests.
> I love the awkward black girls and the quirky black girls and the black girls who listen to punk music.
> I love the "standing at the bus stop, sucking on a lollipop" 'round the way girls.
> Black womanhood—with its unique histories and experiences—marks its possessors as something special.
> I love black women, and I want the world to love black women, too.[1]

The complicated history of Black women forces us to examine and address stereotypes, and to consider the root cause of each of them. This chapter will focus on the history and negative effects of the Jezebel, Mammy, and Sapphire tropes.

JEZEBEL

Jezebel was a biblical figure; we find her in the Hebrew Bible book of First Kings. Jezebel was a Phoenician princess who ordered the deaths of Israel's prophets and forced idol worship upon the people. She eventually met her demise by being thrown from a window and eaten by dogs. Before her assassin arrived, however, she dressed in finery, makeup, and a fancy wig, which contributes to the idea of Jezebel as a seductress or "painted woman." Jezebel has come to symbolize a domineering trickster who uses her sexuality to wreak havoc on men and the world.

From the days of slavery, Jezebel's name has been invoked to describe Black women's alleged unbridled and unprincipled sexuality, animalistic sexual ways, and the pursuit of the white man. This stereotype is especially

---

1. Winfrey Harris, *Sisters Are Alright*, xi.

abominable because enslaved Black women endured savage sexual exploitation and abuse at the hands of white men. This truth makes the Jezebel stereotype an exercise in victim blaming.

On the abject sexual abuses of slavery, Carolyn M. West writes: "[Black women] were placed on the auction block, stripped naked, and examined to determine their reproductive capacity . . . they were coerced, bribed, induced, seduced, ordered and of course, violently forced to have sexual relations with slaveholders . . . the Ku Klux Klan, whipped African Americans, destroyed their property and savagely raped Black women."[2] The white response to these atrocities was to invent the Jezebel stereotype: if Black women always desired depraved sex, they were in essence "unrapeable." The unjust Jezebel stereotype has affected not only the way Black women have been treated by white men but has also led to their abuse by white women as well as a damaged view of their own sexuality.

The slave narrative *Incidents in the Life of a Slave Girl* details the sexual abuse Harriet Jacobs experienced. She sheds light on the ways in which Black women's exploitation has been historically twisted into sinister Jezebel behavior instead of vulnerable victimization.[3] Jacobs's master, Dr. Flint, aggressively pursued Jacobs from the time she was quite young. "No animal ever watched its prey more narrowly than he watched me."[4] In the journal article "Raping the Jezebel: Hypocrisy, Stereotyping, and Sexual Identity in Harriet Jacob's Incidents in the Life of a Slave Girl," Aisha Matthews notes the way that white men attempted to paint such sexual encounters as natural, even expecting enslaved women to show gratitude for their advances. This attitude was based on the idea that Black women could not be virtuous. These sexual exploits by white men aroused jealousy in their wives, who also then turned to the Jezebel stereotype to demonize enslaved women while excusing the behavior of their husbands. This jealousy also led to increased cruelty from female mistresses toward enslaved women.[5]

Jacobs's view of her sexuality is sadly distorted by the idea of "the cult of true womanhood," a white ideal of femininity and virtue that could never be achieved by Black women. Jacobs anguished over her chastity and honor as a Christian woman. She was not allowed to marry a Black man because of Dr. Flint's obsession. Because of this, she then turned to another

2. West, "Mammy, Jezebel, and Sapphire," 294.

3. Jacobs, *Incidents in the Life of a Slave Girl.*

4. Ibid., 39.

5 Matthews, "Raping the Jezebel," 4, 7.

older white suitor, whose advances were still problematic, yet lacked the direct yoke of slavery placed on Jacobs by Flint. This sexual relationship also brought Jacobs anguish because of the obvious power imbalance and her sense of lost virtue. Jacobs made the best choices she could under her oppressive circumstances. She began life as a girl subjected to sexual degradation and ended up as a woman who could never have access to the "cult of true womanhood."

The old notion of the Jezebel appears in modern society as the stereotype of the Welfare Queen. This invidious stereotype appeared around the Reagan era, when he told the story of the notorious Linda Taylor, a career criminal who defrauded the government out of hundreds of thousands of dollars in welfare benefits. Taylor was also a kidnapper, a bigamist, and linked to a mysterious death. Though herself racially ambiguous, her outlandish tale became the source of one of the most pervasive tropes of all time: the lazy, Black, inner city Welfare Queen.[6] The Welfare Queen links pregnancy and motherhood to the stereotype of the scheming Jezebel. If poor, uneducated, single Black women considered unfit to parent become pregnant for the sole purpose of stealing from the government, they have used their sexuality to scheme against virtuous, hard-working white Americans. Updated from the days of slavery to the industrialized age, the Welfare Queen represents the same unjust trope used to judge and marginalize all Black women.

Another modern iteration of the Jezebel is the Video Vixen or "groupie." Usually a woman of color, these women use their overt sexual wiles to seduce rich and famous men to take their money. The Video Vixen stereotype is often perpetuated and internalized within the Black community, demonstrating that the stereotypes placed on Black women have detrimental effects from both inside and outside of the Black community.

MAMMY

Unlike the cunning and seductive Jezebel, the Mammy is a fat, jolly, and compliant Black woman. Covered in earlier chapters, this stereotype rests on the ways in which Black women have been forced to work in domestic service to white families. Mammy is a caricature of a beloved slave who is

---

6. Taylor and her family are listed as white on their birth certificates. However, she acted as a racial chameleon throughout her life, passing for Black, Asian, and Jewish. See Demby, "Original Welfare Queen," lines 23–30.

grateful for her position, loves caring for "the Massa's children," and is not a sexual threat to the mistress.[7] Mammy's family is of no consequence; she exists to happily serve the white household.

Mammy is defined by her appearance as dark skinned, kinky haired (though she is usually kerchiefed), and obese. Because of this, these physical characteristics may be sources of low self-esteem for real women. For Black women, to be large, dark, and "nappy haired" is to fulfill this harmful stereotype. While the traits themselves are not negative, they have been perceived as such by white beauty standards. The negative perception of the mammy body type has also led to issues of body image, disordered eating, and exacerbated weight for Black women.[8]

For modern women, Mammy's legacy brings the newer stereotype of the "Strong Black Woman," superhuman in what she can bear regarding work and caregiving without regard for her own needs. For Black women, "role strain" is a common and frequent threat to health and well-being. There is a belief from both within and outside of the Black community that the Black woman is supposed to be infinitely strong. Coupled with the stresses of systemic racism, classism, and sexism, negative health effects are not uncommon.[9] Anger is also a natural consequence. Black women's anger, however, is another complexity attached to another negative stereotype that Black women bear: the Sapphire.

SAPPHIRE

The sassy Black woman. Everyone has heard of her and has certainly seen her in movies and on television. In fact, we now see her frequently cast as herself in reality television. While mainstream pop culture has attempted to color the Black woman's sass an amusing trait, this problematic concept is deeply entrenched in the American psyche. A loud, back-talking, dark-skinned Black woman is a Sapphire, and she has haunted and limited Black women for generations. The term is named for Sapphire Stevens, the loud, sassy, trash-talking, dark-skinned character from the *Amos and Andy* radio and television shows. The Sapphire's main objective is to nag, criticize, and chastise the weak and bumbling Black men in her life. Often angry, the

7. Green, "Negative Racial Stereotypes," lines 143–50. See also Jewell, *From Mammy to Miss America*, 39.

8. West, "Mammy, Sapphire, and Jezebel," 459.

9. Ibid., 460.

Sapphire seeks to emasculate Black men as often as possible, usually for the amusement of white onlookers. This trope has endured into the twenty-first century under the name of the "Angry Black Woman."

When Barack Obama began his first presidential run, the media placed the Angry Black Woman stereotype on his wife, Michelle. Michelle's commentary on systemic racism in America angered her critics, causing them to quickly brand her as angry. Her anger, they posited, was wholly unjustified because of her relative privilege as a well-educated, financially successful person. Curiously, even Black conservatives criticized and stereotyped the first lady. In 2008, chairman of the National Leadership Network of Black Conservatives-Project 21 Mychal Massie said this: "Compared to the eloquent grace of Jackie Kennedy, Nancy Reagan, Barbara Bush and yes, even Rosalind Carter, she portrays herself as just another angry Black harridan who spits in the face of the nation that made her rich, famous and prestigious."[10] In social media, Michelle is frequently called ugly, mannish, or even a cross-dressing man. She has received criticized as overweight, despite her svelte appearance and apparent physical fitness. The Obamas' critics have gone to great lengths to make Michelle fit into the negative Sapphire stereotype. Even as first lady of the United States, Michelle Obama cannot join the "cult of true womanhood."

The Angry Black Woman also appears frequently on reality television. From *The Real Housewives of Atlanta* to *The Maury Povich Show*, Black women are often shown behaving as the Sapphire stereotype in the media. Until recently, most portrayals of Black women fit into one of the stereotypes frequently attached to Black women. Whether a loud and uncouth woman seeking the paternity of her child, a women behaving badly by arguing loudly in public venues, or more subtle portrayals of the sexless, sassy Black friend, the Sapphire image dominates media representations of Black women to this day.

The Sapphire stereotype also has negative health consequences for Black women. With society discouraging Black women to express anger in an appropriate way, women may develop both mental and physical health problems, like hypertension.[11]

---

10. Parlett, *Demonizing a President*, 89.
11. West, "Mammy, Jezebel, and Sapphire," 461.

AN OPPOSITIONAL GAZE

Black feminist scholar bell hooks responds to the onslaught of negative, stereotypical portrayals of Black women by calling for Black women to view such portrayals with an "oppositional gaze."[12] This gaze may be defined in two ways. First, hooks identifies the way which Black people have historically been denied the right to look white counterparts in the eye. To do so was a dangerous exercise during the times of slavery and Jim Crow. This aspect of the oppositional gaze allows Black people to confront white people by looking them in the eye. The second aspect of the oppositional gaze focuses on the ways Blacks have been forced to view themselves and their white counterparts in art and media. Black women have had no choice but to be consumers of media that relies on negative stereotypes of Black women and simultaneously presents an unobtainable version of white femininity and desirability.[13] For hooks, the oppositional gaze gives Black women the ability to challenge negative stereotypes and resist racist depictions of womanhood.[14]

Black women's experiences are heavily laden with the legacy of slavery, intersectional oppression, and stereotyping. This experience spans from the big screen to the academy to the church pulpit. Based on the experiences of Black women in slavery and beyond, there is much baggage to be carried as we create our theology and examine the ways in which we fit into theology. Womanist theological pursuits begin with the sometimes dark and always complex history of Black womanhood. One cannot understand womanism without understanding the history and cultural concepts laid out in the first section of this book. Now we turn to a woman who also lived a deep and complex experience, centuries before African-American women reached our shores and centuries before she was coopted by the "cult of true womanhood": Mary, mother of Jesus.

12. Hooks, "Oppositional Gaze," 115.
13. Ibid., 117.
14. Ibid., 122.

PART 2

TRADITIONAL MARIOLOGY

4

A MARIOLOGY PRIMER

Since the days of the early church, Christians have engaged in the study of Mary and her role in Christian theology. Scholarship regarding Mary is aptly named Mariology. From the earliest Christian theological debates to the encyclicals by the most recent popes, Marian studies have endured. Predictably, most of this scholarship takes place in the Roman Catholic tradition.[1] However, with the rise of feminist scholarship as well as an increasing spiritual interest in the divine feminine, Mary is slowly appearing in Protestant theological studies as well.

When considering the role of Mariology in postmodernity, it is crucial to have an understanding of Mariology throughout Christian history. Just as Christology has undergone many iterations ranging from the Apostolic Age through the Rationalist Age, Mariology has done the same. In this chapter, I attempt to provide a broad overview of Marian theological thought throughout the ages.

THEOTOKOS: MARY AND THE EARLY CHURCH

In the centuries following the birth of Christianity, the faith went from an alternative religious movement comprised of a small circle of Jewish Jesus-believers to a religion whose influence reached far beyond Judea.

1. While Marian Theology has a rich tradition in the Eastern Orthodox churches, this chapter focuses on Roman Catholic doctrine in contrast with Protestant doctrine. Eastern church theology is discussed for historical context only.

25

The earliest era of the church was known as the Apostolic Age. This period began, as the name suggests, with the twelve apostles of Jesus, starting with the Great Commission given by the resurrected Christ up until the death of the last apostle, John, around the year 100 CE.

As the church moved further away from its beginnings, it was inevitable that different opinions and interpretations of belief would develop. As the reach of the church spread, it became more structured, and believers were followers of church fathers, or patriarchs, who were learned scholars or bishops who wrote and interpreted theology. These patriarchs were responsible for establishing Christian dogma, seeking to create a cohesive orthodoxy for the faith. The patriarchs were divided culturally by region, with a clear split between the Eastern and Western branches of the church. The Eastern church included the Coptic churches of Egypt, the Antiochene church, the Byzantine church, and Ethiopian and Syrian churches, among others. Alternatively, the Western church fathers were physically and philosophically centered in Rome.

One of the most contentious issues amongst early church leadership was establishing an orthodoxy concerning an accurate understanding of the divinity and humanity of Jesus Christ, known as Christology. This conflict was the patristic christological debate between the Nestorius of Constantinople and Cyril of Alexandria. The two men clashed in ideology about the two natures of Jesus. Nestorius held a nuanced view that implied that Jesus was made of two distinct natures, human and divine. Nestorius insisted that God could not be killed on the cross because God, by definition, is eternal and cannot die. Just as God could not die, Nestorius also felt God could not be born of a woman. Therefore, he advocated for calling Mary *Christokos* or "Christ-Bearer," instead of *Theotokos* or "God-Bearer." Cyril vehemently attacked Nestorius's stance, arguing that it improperly separated the humanity and divinity in Jesus, which he held could not be separated. Because of this, Cyril defended the already established tradition of referring to Mary as Theotokos.[2]

The dispute climaxed at the Council of Ephesus in 431 CE. The doctrine endorsed by the politically powerful Cyril prevailed as Nestorius was excommunicated, along with any reluctance to name Mary as the mother of God. The council reaffirmed the contents of the Nicene Creed, which was first created at the Council of Nicea in 325 CE and revised at the Council of Constantinople in 381 CE. During the the patristic councils, Mary's role

2. Outler, "Christ in Christian Tradition," 450–52.

as Theotokos was debated, but belief in Mary's virgin birth of Jesus was never questioned. By this time, the virgin birth was a well-settled part of Christian dogma, included in the orthodoxy without reservation.

THE QUEST FOR THE HISTORICAL MARY

Theologians have spent decades attempting to learn as much as possible about the historical life of Jesus Christ. The era of scholarship known as the First Quest for the Historical Jesus developed in the nineteenth century. This movement attempted to learn as much as possible about the man we know as Jesus Christ from a historical perspective. Treating Jesus as a historical figure, First Quest scholars tried their best to act as objective historians, not religious theologians.

The first quest came to its pinnacle with the seminal work of German theologian Albert Schweitzer in his book *The Quest of the Historical Jesus*.[3] In his controversial work, Schweitzer endeavored to find a Jesus who is liberated from the baggage of religious tradition, applying a purely historical method to the study of Jesus. Schweitzer's views were starkly different than earlier theologians concerning Jesus because those scholars treated Jesus' divinity as a natural starting point for Christology. What Schweitzer attempted to provide was knowledge of "the real Jesus." The problem with approaching Jesus Christ using the historical method is this: the only source of information we have about Jesus is the Bible. All of what we know about the historical Jesus comes mainly from the four canonical gospels, the book of Acts, and the canonical letters of the apostle Paul. These texts were all written with a retrospective view of Jesus already identified as the Christ. Because of this, all accounts of a post-Easter Jesus were written with the notion that Jesus is the Messiah as a fundamental presupposition.

With our only historical sources as sacred texts, we do not have much hope of constructing a viable objective and historical biography of Jesus. What we know of the historical Jesus is this: He was born around the time we know as year 1. He was born in the region of Galilee and lived in a town called Nazareth. There is nothing reliable about life before he began his public ministry as an adult. Many scholars believe that the details of Jesus' birth story in the Gospels of Matthew and Luke are highly mythological or, at best, highly embellished.

3. See also Awad, "Elaboration on the First Quest."

These unreliable birth narratives are where most of our knowledge of Mary is derived. As a result, we have even less historical information about Mary than we do about Jesus. Mary, as it stands, is historically unknown to us. What has been historically determined about Mary comes from the canonical gospels and the apocryphal *Gospel of James* (which provides a colorful account of Mary's origin story), as well as a hypothetical portrait based on generalities about Jewish life in the region of Galilee around the time when Mary and Jesus lived.

The woman we call Mary of Nazareth was known as Miriam, a Jewish name honoring Miriam, sister of Moses.[4] Miriam was a Jewish woman who was born and most likely lived her entire life in the region of Galilee. Because the birth of her son Jesus happens to be the temporal landmark we use to keep time, we know that she lived during the years before and after what we know as year 1, the beginning of the first century.

We cannot know much historical detail about Miriam of Nazareth other than the fact that she probably existed. To get to know her, we must learn about how life for a woman like her would have been. These historical generalizations will give us a shred of insight into the life of the mother of Jesus. By weaving generalizations together with biblical scholarship, I will attempt to produce a tapestry of a portrait of Mary that will serve as a foundation for our experience with her. The result will not be a photograph, but a rich and imperfect tapestry that illustrates her likeness.

Can Anything Good Come Out of Nazareth?

"We have found him about whom Moses in the law and also the prophets wrote, Jesus son of Joseph from Nazareth." Nathanael said to him, "Can anything good come out of Nazareth?" Philip said to him, "Come and see." (John 1:45–46)

Nazareth was not the home of kings. It was a small Galilean village of little consequence in the ancient world. In fact, there is no mention of the village in the Hebrew Scriptures, so we may assume that it was not a significant

---

4. While Miriam is historically accurate, I choose to use the name Mary throughout this volume because of its significance in the Christian tradition in which womanist theology is located.

influence in Jewish society.[5] Today, Nazareth is the capital of Israel, but we can be fairly certain that in the first century this town was entirely nondescript.

Because of the cultural interest in the origin of Jesus Christ, significant archaeological work has been done in the region of Galilee. Archaeologist Jonathan Reed has been a leading influence in unearthing ancient Galilee.[6] Reed's work in the neighboring Galilean village of Sepphoris gives us reliable information that we may take the liberty of applying to our hypothesis of the way Mary's life in Nazareth would have been. In his exploration, Reed discovered some typical household items like broken pots and kitchen scrap.[7] Reed teaches that much can be gleaned from what was *not* found. For example, there have been no discoveries indicating that running water or sewage systems existed.[8] Reed also notes that when examining these villages archaeologically, there are no signs of protective, defensive walls, public buildings, visual art, or fine household items.[9] There was no sense of gentility here; we can deduce that Nazareth was a poor, meager, smelly place to live.

A young Nazarene woman like Mary would have lived as part of a large peasant class. Peasant families made up about 90 percent of the ancient Gallilean population.[10] This peasant class was perpetually kept from any economic advancement, in part because of the astronomical taxes that they were required to pay to support both the small upper class as well as the Roman state.[11] The social stratification at play in ancient Palestine has been comprehensively presented by American sociologist Gerhard Lenski. Marian scholar Elizabeth A. Johnson provides a concise summary of Lenski's summary of this social stratification.[12] In Lenski's model, several classes existed below the agrarian peasant class. One of these was the artisan class. While today the term "artisan" evokes images of one who carefully crafts well-appreciated items, in Mary's time the artisan class was not so glamorous. Mary was married to a *tekton*, a member of the artisan class, who

5. Johnson, *Truly Our Sister*, 141.

6. Ibid., 139–40.

7. Ibid., 138.

8. Ibid., 142.

9. Ibid., 143.

10. Ibid., 141, 145, 147.

11. Ibid., 148.

12. Ibid., 145; Lenski, *Power and Privilege*, 228.

worked with wood, stonemasonry, or as a cartwright.[13] Beneath a *tekton* existed only people who were unclean and untouchable, like sex workers, beggars, and criminals.[14]

Political Unrest: The Death of Herod the Great

The ruthless despot Herod the Great was appointed king of Judea by the Roman Empire. He ruled the region of Judea from around 37 BCE until 4 BCE. According to Elizabeth Johnson, Mary would have grown up under Herod's violent reign and was likely a young mother to Jesus when Herod died.[15] As Mary cared for her infant in the midst of turmoil, both she and her baby lived in a time of great insecurity and danger.

Jesus was born into poverty, in a time of unrest and domestic terror. His mother was young, poor, and unmarried at the time she became pregnant and gave birth. Historical context makes it clear that Mary was a young woman living a highly marginalized existence, representative of the "least" of people. As a vulnerable young mother, Mary's reality was similar to the lives of many young women who live on the fringes today.

THE MARIAN CULT

One of the greatest sources of Protestant trepidation regarding Mary is the fear of treading into the territory of idolatrous worship of Mary. Many Protestants are reluctant to consider any role of Mary in the Christian practice because of a strong disapproval of the Catholic treatment of the mother of Jesus. Salvation is to be earned by faith in Jesus Christ alone, and there is to be no God but the Trinity; the Father, Son Jesus, and the Holy Spirit. Mary, nor any other person, has any business in the equation.

While some Protestants may have a knowledge of current Catholic doctrine regarding Mary, many are put off by the mysterious history of the Marian cult. First, let us consider the loaded nature of the term "cult." In popular culture, the word evokes images of doomsday groups with dangerous leaders. The term "cult" is laden with much negativity in the vernacular.

13. Johnson, *Truly Our Sister*, 147.

14. Ibid., 146.

15. In the passages immediately following his account of Herod's death, Josephus describes sedition against his successor, Archelaus. Josephus, *Jewish Antiquities*, book 17, ch. 9.

However, in religious history, the word has not always had such a nefarious meaning.

The Latin for cult, *cultus*, is translated as "care" or "adoration."[16] "Cult" has historically been used to describe a movement of veneration or devotion directed towards a particular figure. Several Catholic documents refer to Marian devotion as the "Marian cult," such as Paul VI's papal encyclical titled *Marialis Cultus*. Armed with this definition, we may move away from images of dangerous fringe groups and toward the history of the cult surrounding Mary in the early church.

> You also see and hear that not only in Ephesus but in almost the whole of Asia this Paul has persuaded and drawn away a considerable number of people by saying that gods made with hands are not gods. And there is danger not only that this trade of ours may come into disrepute but also that the temple of the great goddess Artemis will be scorned, and she will be deprived of her majesty that brought all Asia and the world to worship her." When they heard this, they were enraged and shouted, "Great is Artemis of the Ephesians!" (Acts 19:26–28)

> In torchlit processions through the city, the Ephesians demonstrated their jubilation that the man who had slighted the Virgin Mary had been deposed. "Praise be to the *Theotokos*! Long live Cyril!" they cheered.[17]

Paul's traveling ministry took him into a pagan world that was familiar with the practice of goddess worship, as displayed by this passage in Acts. The Ephesians' held rancor toward Paul because of their commitment to their goddess Artemis. Because of this, it stands to reason that the Hellenic influence on the early church would bring with it an emphasis on practices that bridged the gap between their previous beliefs and their new ones. With the rise of Christianity in the Roman Empire, it was not a far leap for the Gentile church to eventually replace their lady Artemis with a new lady in Mary.

Scholars disagree on whether the Marian cult was first active during the fourth century before the major church councils occurred, or not until the fifth century in reaction to the councils declaring that Mary's proper

16. *Merriam-Webster*, s.v. "cultus." https://www.merriam-webster.com/dictionary/cultus.

17. Warner, *Alone of All Her Sex*, 65.

title is Theotokos.[18] However, evidence of Marian devotion reaches as far back as the second century with the creation of the *Gospel of James*.[19] This gospel provides a colorful account of Mary's origin story, focusing on her experiences and not her son's.[20]

Epiphanius, the patriarch of Constantinople, wrote in criticism of a sect of female worshippers known as the Collyridians, who appointed women as priests and observed the custom of leaving bread, cakes, and spirits at the shrine formerly devoted to Ashtaroth, goddess of heaven.[21] Ancient Easterners had engaged in goddess worship for generations, which Epiphanius points out in his rebuke of the Collyridian women. In her work *Alone of All Her Sex: The Myth and the Cut of the Virgin Mary*, Marina Warner notes that the practice of giving offerings to Ashtaroth was also reviled by the prophet Jeremiah in the Hebrew Scriptures.[22] Warner details several connections of Mary with pagan goddess symbolism, with an emphasis on her connection to the celebration of fertility, birth, and marriage. Elizabeth Johnson also provides examples of the link between veneration of the Virgin and pagan goddess worship. For instance, Johnson examines the early Syriac church's use of the image of a mother bird, stretching her protective wings, as a favored image of the Holy Spirit. Johnson states that the Spirit's outstretched wings eventually evolved into an image of Mary with an outstretched cloak, protecting her children beneath her symbolic wings.[23]

The Marian cult also gave birth to the idea of Mary as Queen of Heaven. The image of Mary as queen adorned with a precious crown comes from her coronation as queen after she was assumed into heaven.[24] In *Alone of All Her Sex*, Warner posits that though the adoration of Mary as queen was sincerely held, the choice to appoint her royal status was no coincidence. By placing Mary in a position as a bejeweled queen, she reinforced the idea of reverence and obedience to the theocracy that existed in Rome.[25]

One of the best-known depictions of Mary as a queen is that of the Black Madonna of Częstochowa, who in 1652 was crowned as queen and

18. Shoemaker, "Cult in the Fourth Century."

19. Warner, *Alone of All Her Sex*, 347.

20. Chapter 5 of this volume includes a deeper analysis of the *Gospel of James*.

21. Warner, *Alone of All Her Sex*, 275.

22. Ibid.

23. Johnson, *Truly Our Sister*, 78–79.

24. The assumption will be discussed in more detail later in this chapter.

25. Warner, *Alone of All Her Sex*, 104.

protector of Poland. The icon was offered crowns by several royals and members of the nobility. These jewels as well as others have been placed upon her crown over time, heavily adorning the icon. The image holds a sort of royal court daily, as a screen rises to reveal her to her waiting subjects several times a day.

In addition to her titles of Queen of Heaven and Theotokos, over the years Mary has also been called Mediatrix. In his work *Mary Through the Centuries: Her Place in the History of Culture*, Jaroslav Pelikan discusses the relationship between the twelfth- and thirteenth-century view connecting Mary as Mater Dolorosa, or "Mother of Sorrows," to her role as Mediatrix.[26] The idea focused on the tension existing between Mary's role as a grieving mother and her role in standing bravely at the cross welcoming her son's death as her savior and the savior of the world.[27] Pelikan teaches that the title "Mediatrix of law and grace" originated in the Eastern church. The role of Mediatrix was historically defined in at least two ways. One way is by existing as one who takes requests for mercy from her son, acting in mediation between believers and Christ. A second and more nuanced interpretation (which likely has greater ecumenical appeal) is that Mary served as a mediator by receiving Jesus into her womb and birthing him into the world; her physical act of motherhood mediated God into his human form.[28] Mary's mediation of graces is available especially to those most in need, which may be thought of as "the least."

After centuries of thriving prominently within the Roman Catholic and Orthodox traditions, the birth of Martin Luther, an excommunicated reformer, led to the rise of a Christian movement that would change the view of Mary forever. In the Protestant Reformation, titles like Mediatrix became especially repugnant, as did the idea of the Marian cult in its entirety. This new era for Mary would look very different than her past, eventually influencing her role in the Catholic Church as well.

LUTHER ON MARY

While Martin Luther was the father of the Protestant Reformation, he was born into the late medieval Catholic Church with all that it entailed, including the Marian cult. In fact, Luther's call to the religious life was inspired

26. Pelikan, *Mary Through the Centuries*, 125–26.
27. Ibid.
28. Ibid., 130.

by an experience as a boy: he prayed fervently to St. Anne, asking for her protection from a storm, bargaining that in return for her protection he would become a monk.[29] Born in 1483, Luther's faith formed in a church where the intercession of saints was common, and where Mary was the greatest and most frequently called upon of the saints.

Luther's most well-known and complete treatise on Mary is his 1521 commentary on the Magnificat. In this work, Luther focused on a view of Mary steeped only in her humility and obedience, while denying that she was somehow worthy of her grace or in some way higher than other mere humans. Luther writes, "Mary does not desire to be an idol; she does nothing, God does all."[30] This view of Mary, which focused solely on her humanity, humility, and lowliness, warned against the overuse of the title Queen of Heaven, which bestowed praise unto Mary that was only due to the Godhead himself.

Donal Flannigan examines Luther's criticism of "false singers" of the Magnificat, of which Luther tells us there are two sorts: those who only praise God when he blesses them well, and those who magnify themselves and their own image and actions above those of God. These criticisms support the disapproval of the over-elevation of Mary, because, as stated, Mary would not want such treatment. She as a model of faith who knew better than to fall into these self-indulgent traps.

In the end, however, when writing his commentary on the Magnificat, Luther was a product of his late medieval paradigm, which resulted in his retention of a somewhat nuanced view of certain core aspects of Marian doctrine, such as his defense of perpetual virginity and his nuanced view regarding the immaculate conception of Mary.[31] It was the later 1537 Smalcald Articles that took a more direct attack on the invocation of saints, teaching that the practice "is neither commanded nor recommended, has to precedent in the Scripture."[32]

The tension between Protestants and Catholics created by Luther and his adherents persisted as Christianity continued to develop in post-medieval contexts. With an awareness of this tension as well as an awareness of the enduring influence of the Protestant church on Christianity, the Catholic Church became concerned with matters of ecumenism. This

29. Kreitzer, "Luther Regarding the Virgin Mary," 252.
30. Luther, *Annotated Luther*, vol. 4, 350.
31. Kreitzer, "Luther Regarding the Virgin Mary," 261–62.
32. Ibid., 253.

ecumenical approach was apparent when Catholic leadership convened to reaffirm their doctrine for the modern world at Vatican II.

MODERN CATHOLIC MARIAN THEOLOGY

The Second Vatican Ecumenical Council (commonly known as Vatican II) began in 1962 and lasted through several periods, concluding in 1965. During the council, Roman Catholic leadership engaged in a rigorous debate regarding the state of the twentieth-century Catholic Church and its doctrine. The topic of Marian dogma was a source of serious contention; however, at the council's conclusion, the Church emerged with the doctrine regarding Mary that they hold today.

Vatican II occurred during a wave of interest in ecumenism in the Catholic Church. Naturally, Marian doctrine was of concern in this regard, as a significant point of divergence existing between Catholics and Protestants. The document *Lumen Gentium*, produced by the council in 1964, provided a careful balance of emphasizing the uniqueness of Jesus' role as redeemer and mediator. However, the document also included a statement that supported the cult of the Blessed Virgin in the Church insofar as it did not amount to the level of adoration that is offered to the Son as well as to the Father and the Holy Spirit.[33]

In addition to her well-established role as Theotokos, Vatican II doctrine focuses mainly on these topics: Mary's immaculate conception, assumption into heaven, perpetual virginity, and queenship of heaven and the church. The council also tempered the Church's stance on Mary as Mediatrix.

Immaculate Conception

In 1954, Pope Pius IX's encyclical *Ineffabilis Deus* solidified Mary's immaculate conception into Catholic dogma. Pius IX cites the apostolic predecessors who established a strong tradition of honoring the conception of Mary, which was well known to have occurred without what he called

---

33. Paul IV, *Lumen Gentium*, ch. 8, sec. 4, para. 66.

"hereditary taint.[34] The Vatican II council affirmed Pius IX in its statement *Lumen Gentium,* referring to the Mary as the "Immaculate Virgin."[35]

The Assumption

For many years, members of the Catholic Church and clergy held the belief that at the end of her earthly life Mary was assumed into heaven. The idea of the assumption of Mary can be found as far back as the fourth century, when Eastern patriarch Epiphanius of Salamis wrote his *Panarion.*[36] Epiphanius himself was unsure if she died a natural death before being taken, writing that "no one knows her end.[37] Epiphanius did, however, later make a direct comparison between Mary and the prophet Elijah, writing that "she is like Elijah, who was virgin from his mother's womb, always remained so, and was taken up, but has not seen death."[38]

In 1950, Pope Pius XII formally defined the Roman Catholic doctrine of the assumption:

> By the authority of our Lord Jesus Christ, of the Blessed Apostles Peter and Paul, and by our own authority, we pronounce, declare, and define it to be a divinely revealed dogma: that the Immaculate Mother of God, the ever Virgin Mary, having completed the course of her earthly life, was assumed body and soul into heavenly glory.[39]

Pius XII's declaration was later supported by the Vatican II statement *Lumen Gentium*: "The Immaculate Virgin, preserved free from all guilt of original sin on the completion of her earthly sojourn, was taken up body and soul into heavenly glory."[40]

Today Mary's assumption is commemorated by a feast day in August, which is celebrated worldwide. A popular celebration of the feast of the assumption is held annually in Cleveland's Little Italy neighborhood.

---

34. Pius IX, *Ineffablis Deus*, para. 44. Pius IX specifically names Sixtus IV, Paul V, and Gregory XV, with Sixtus IV writing on the immaculate conception as early as 1476.

35. Paul VI, *Lumen Gentium*, ch. 8, sec. 2, para. 59.

36. Epiphanius, *Panarion.*

37. Ibid., 79.23.8 (p. 635).

38. Ibid., 79.5.1 (p. 641).

39. Pius XII, *Munificentissiums Deus*, para. 44.

40. Paul VI, *Lumen Gentium*, ch. 8, sec. 2, para. 59.

Perpetual Virginity

Mary's perpetual virginity is another Marian doctrine that has endured for ages. Before Vatican II, Pope Pius XII wrote on the consecrated virginity of Mary, reaffirming the permanent condition of her virginity in his 1954 encyclical *Sacra Virginitas*.[41] Likewise, Vatican II spoke of the importance of the sanctity of Mary's perpetual virginity. *Lumen Gentium* declares that the birth of Christ"[D]id not diminish His mother's virginal integrity but sanctified it."[42] Throughout the document, the council refers to the established doctrine that Mary was "ever-virgin."[43]

Today, the Catholic Catechism teaches that Mary is ever-virgin, and addresses the common question regarding references to Jesus' brothers and sisters in the New Testament, which would seemingly negate Mary's perpetual virginity. The Catechism teaches that belief in the virgin condition of Mary is a matter of faith, and explains Jesus' brothers and sisters as close relatives, referencing the Old Testament use of the term "brother" in this manner.[44]

Mediatrix Mitigated, Queenship Affirmed

Vatican II's quest for an ecumenical approach placed emphasis on Mary as a model of the Christian faith instead of Mediatrix. Elizabeth Johnson tells us that Mary's Vatican II role as Mediatrix was "relativized" in three ways: (1) by placing the title amongst a row of other titles; (2) by placing the title in a merely descriptive context regarding Marian piety rather than a prescriptive doctrinal context; and (3) most importantly, by providing language that provides a serious caveat that any mediating role of Mary is to be viewed as highly inferior to that of her son.[45] In keeping with the ecumenical focus of this Marian relativism, Vatican II emphasized Mary's role as a model of Christian faith and virtue, making her perhaps the first and most perfect Christian.

Unlike Luther's disdain for Mary's title as the Queen of Heaven, the Catholic Church embraces the title of Queen of Heaven as one that Mary

---

41. Pius XII, *Sacra Virginitas*.

42. Paul VI, *Lumen Gentium*, ch. 8, sec. 2, para. 57.

43. Ibid., paras. 50, 52, 57, 69.

44. USCCB, *Catechism of the Catholic Church*, 144.

45. Johnson, *Truly Our Sister*, 130.

deserves as a model Christian and the highest of the saints. The encyclical *Ad Caeli Reginam*, written in Pius XII's 1954 series of Marian writings, solidified Mary's office as Queen of Heaven, and Queen of both the Catholic Church as well as the church universal. In the opening of his letter, Pius XII states, "Mary, the Virgin Mother of God, reigns with a mother's solicitude over the entire world, just as she is crowned in heavenly blessedness with the glory of a Queen."[46] *Lumen Gentium* awards Mary the title Queen of the Universe.

Since the birth of the poor Nazarene girl named Miriam around the beginning of the first century, Mary has been exalted and diminished by countless religious leaders, theologians, and lay Christians alike. The early church councils and the Marian cult are the sources of much of the Mariology we consider today. However, the New Testament tells us very little about Miriam. The time we spend with her in the Scriptures is precious little. To build a biblical foundation for a womanist Mariology, we must carefully consider the Scriptures.

46. Pius XII, *Ad Caeli Reginam*, para. 1.

5

THE BIBLICAL MARY

While Mary appears in each of the four canonical gospels, the totality of biblical scripture about Mary is quite scant. Because of the small amount of Marian material in the Christian scriptures, we will address Mary's depiction and role in each of the four canonical gospels. The gospels tell us virtually all we know of Jesus. As a consequence, they also teach us all we know about Mary.

AN UNFLATTERING DEPICTION: MARY IN THE GOSPEL ACCORDING TO MARK

> Then his mother and his brothers came; and standing outside, they sent to him and called him. A crowd was sitting around him; and they said to him, "Your mother and your brothers and sisters are outside asking for you." And he replied, "Who are my mother and brothers?" And looking at those who sat around him, he said, "Here are my mother and my brothers! Whoever does the will of God is my brother and sister and mother." (Mark 3:31–35)

The Gospel according to Mark is considered by most scholars to be the earliest written gospel, placing its composition around the year 70 CE, when the Romans destroyed the Jerusalem temple, making it an important temporal landmark in Jewish history. The temple was the center of Jewish religious worship, the place where Jews went to offer their sacrifices of atonement each year. It also housed the holy of holies, the innermost and most sacred part of the temple. This place housed the ark of the covenant. Only the high priest could enter this place, and only once a year, on Yom Kippur.

The violence in Jerusalem in 70 CE represented to an apocalyptic scenario. Followers of Christ believed that the Son of Man had come in anticipation of the impending end of days. Mark is the shortest canonical gospel. It has a hurried pace and succinct nature that echoes the war-torn context of its time. Therefore, we may imagine that the evangelist who wrote the gospel chose his details carefully, and with the goal of boosting the moral of the early Jerusalem church during difficult times.

In Mark 3:31–35, Jesus encounters his mother and brothers, and does not give them a warm greeting; in fact, he does not address them at all. The text makes it clear that Jesus' mother and brothers came to find him. They are outsiders, quite literally outside of the circle where Jesus sat. When the disciples announced their presence, Jesus does not react to the news with a cheerful instruction to bring them in. Instead, he uses this situation as what Elizabeth Struthers Malbon in the Women's Bible Commentary calls a "teachable moment."[1] Jesus does not acknowledge his family; he only uses the opportunity to teach his followers that they are now his mothers and brothers. It is not difficult to imagine such a reaction breaking a mother's heart, especially when her son is a political and religious agitator with many enemies.

We may read this scene in Mark as an indication that Jesus and his family were estranged. However, since Jesus often used parables and metaphors, perhaps this vignette can be interpreted another way. Mark's author knew that the early church was hurting and in a state of tumult. The church's families may have been injured or killed by the violence. Alternatively, relatives may have rejected their faith in Jesus as heretical. By stating that his followers were his family, Jesus provided comfort to his people by issuing an invitation into what Paul would later name "the Body of Christ."

At face value, however, this passage depicts Mary as a mother seeking out her son. We know Jesus' reaction because he speaks in the passage. Unfortunately, Mary remains outside the door, silent. All we know is that she wanted to see her son.

1. Malbon, "Gospel of Mark," 482.

THE SON OF MARY

"Is not this the carpenter, the son of Mary and brother of James and Joseph and Judas and Simon, and are not his sisters here with us?" And they took offense at him. (Mark 6:3)

In biblical times, social protocol identified people as the child of his or her father. Here, we see people referring to Jesus as the son of Mary. This statement likely had some negative implications.

Mark does not include a birth narrative. There is no annunciation; we as readers do not witness the angel Gabriel coming to Mary, telling her that the Holy Spirit will make her pregnant. Because of that, we enter a story of Jesus with a mother, but without mention of a father. Was Joseph the putative father? Was the story of Jesus' miraculous conception considered common knowledge, rendering a birth narrative unnecessary? Or was Jesus, the Messiah, known as illegitimate? Was Mary regarded as a fallen woman who bore a bastard child?

In the two brief encounters with Mary in the Gospel according to Mark, she is certainly not depicted with high regard or any concern at all. As the Jesus movement continued to develop, Mary got more attention in later gospels through the introduction of the birth narrative.

THE PROPHECY FULFILLED: THE BIRTH NARRATIVE IN MATTHEW

The Gospel according to Matthew is known as the most Jewish of the gospels. The author of this gospel pays great attention to connecting the details of the life of Jesus with the prophecies of the Hebrew Bible. Matthew's audience was the Jewish community, whom the evangelist was attempting to convince of Jesus' messianic significance.

The case for the Messiah begins with a detailed genealogy spanning from Abraham to King David to Joseph, husband of Mary. The fact that this genealogy traces the lineage of Joseph and not Mary is curious since Joseph is not purported to be the natural father of Jesus. However, the provision of the Davidic line lays a foundation for Matthew's messianic focus, as the Jewish community was awaiting a Messiah descended from King David.

In Matthew, we encounter Joseph fretting over what to do with the already pregnant Mary. He has a dream in which God informs him that the child Mary is carrying was conceived by the Holy Spirit, a message that Joseph accepts and which eliminates his reluctance to wed Mary.

Mary plays no significant role in Matthew beyond her virginal conception and birth of Jesus, which fulfilled a prophecy given by Isaiah that forete that the Messiah would be born of a virgin. Isaiah 7:14 states, "Therefore the Lord himself will give you a sign. Look, the young woman is with child and shall bear a son, and shall name him Immanuel." While the NRSV refers to a "young woman," a footnote indicates that the original Greek in this verse may also mean "virgin." For this prophecy in Isaiah we fine fulfillment in the virgin Mary.

MAGNIFICAT: LUKE'S PORTRAIT OF MARY

The evangelist who gives us the detailed account of the Gospel of Luke paints the most detailed picture of Mary. In his gospel, Mary, along with her kinswoman Elizabeth, take center stage by receiving prophecies and miraculous births. Luke portrays Mary's encounter with the angel Gabriel in great detail. From Gabriel's jubilant salutation, "Greetings, favored one! The Lord is with you" (1:28), to Mary's awestruck response to his message, readers receive the most satisfying view of Mary in the canonical gospels. After the annunciation, Mary travels into the hill country to visit Elizabeth.

Luke gives us Mary's famous song of praise known as the Magnificat.[2] In this song, Mary expresses her joy upon accepting God's charge to carry and give birth to the Savior. She also focuses on the power of God to raise her and her community up from their low social position.

Luke gives readers a glimpse of Mary's state of mind by referencing the way in which she "treasured" and "pondered" her unique experience as Jesus' mother. These private experiences are shared with readers in the nativity scene when shepherds arrive to praise the baby Jesus, and also when the young Jesus spends time with the teachers in the temple, which he refers to as his "Father's house." Jesus is no ordinary boy, a fact that Mary treasures and ponders in her heart.

Chapter 2 of the gospel tells of the prophecy given by a man named Simeon, who encounters the child Jesus outside of the temple. Simeon foretells of Jesus' important role to come. Simeon also astutely prophesies that Mary's soul will be pierced by a sword in the process, alluding to the pain she would experience as she watched her son suffer on the cross.

2. See chapter 11 of this volume for a more detailed analysis of the Magnificat.

FROM CANA TO THE CROSS: MARY IN THE GOSPEL ACCORDING TO JOHN

The non-synoptic Gospel of John is the place where the early church moves away from the apostolic accounts of Christ to develop a distinct Christology. Scholars usually date John anywhere between 95 and 100 CE and hold that the work comes from an early church group excluded from Jewish temple life.

The Gospel of John gives us a much more elevated version of the incarnated Christ, or what might be called a Christology "from above." In other words, there is no doubt to the writer, the reader, or the people living within the gospel that Jesus was born, lived, and died as Messiah. His mother, Mary, knew he was special from the start, as shown to us in the depiction of Jesus' first sign at the wedding in Cana:

> When the wine gave out, the mother of Jesus said to him, 'They have no wine." And Jesus said to her, "Woman, what concern is that to you and to me? My hour has not yet come." His mother said to the servants, "Do whatever he tells you." (John 2:3–5)

This account shows a young Jesus who is acutely aware of his power and divinity. Moreover, his mother, Mary, also knows very well that her son has miraculous capabilities. What it also shows us is that Mary is ready for the world to behold her son's capabilities.

Upon a close reading, Mary sees this wine dilemma as the proper catalyst for Jesus to show those around him that he is not an ordinary boy. Mary says directly to Jesus that the wine has run out. While this may be an annoyed observation by the average thirsty wedding guest, Mary speaks with a sense of knowing. She does not need to tell Jesus what she is thinking. Jesus then pushes back; according to his timeline, his time has not yet come. However, mother Mary then springs into action by telling the people to do whatever Jesus says. She is ready for Jesus to reveal himself through this sign. It is clear that Mary has a true belief in Jesus' divinity, and that it is time he shares his gifts with the world. Mary urges Jesus to perform a lavish sign, providing a copious amount of good wine. There is more wine than there was before, and it is of better quality. By offering this gesture of radical hospitality through the wedding wine, the gospel also foreshadows the ultimate gesture of grace that he will offer to the world through his blood.

STABAT MATER: STANDING AT THE CROSS

> Meanwhile, standing near the cross of Jesus were his mother, and
> his mother's sister, Mary the wife of Clopas, and Mary Magdalene.
> When Jesus saw his mother and the disciple whom he loved stand-
> ing beside her, he said to his mother, "Woman, here is your son."
> Then he said to the disciple, "Here is your mother." And from that
> hour the disciple took her into his own home. (John 19:26–27)

At the crucifixion, the Gospel of John tells of four women named Mary
standing at the cross as Jesus dies his slow and agonizing death. Mary, the
mother of Jesus, endures this tragic experience. She watches her son tortured to death at the hands of Israel's foreign occupiers. Mary has no re-
course. John illustrates Mary mothering Jesus in the way that we most often
imagine—with fervent belief, respect, and devotion. The high christological outlook in the Gospel of John leads the way for a future non-canonical
gospel that would embellish Mary's role in Christ's story. This was done
in a way that exhibited the growing Marian cult that existed in the early
Christian community.

BEYOND THE CANON: MARY IN THE GOSPEL
OF JAMES

During the first three centuries of early Christianity, the church established
the New Testament canon. After several church councils, the twenty-seven
books that we now know as the New Testament were selected as canonical
scripture. This period produced several other gospels, epistles, and apocalyptic works. One of these non-canonical gospels is the *Gospel of James*.
This mid-second-century gospel is also known as the *Protoevangelum of
James* or the *Infancy Gospel of James*.[3]

This gospel expands upon the infancy narratives in the Matthew and
Luke, adding significant back story regarding Jesus' mother. Moreover,
James provides colorful details regarding Mary's personal experiences after
the conception and birth of Infant Jesus.

James gives us a rich and detailed account of Mary's origin story. The
author first introduces Anna, the wife of the wealthy and pious Joachim.
Anna laments her infertility and pleads with God to bless her with a child.

---

3. See chapter 5 for a comparison between the *Gospel of James* and the Surah Maryam
in the Qur'an.

God answers her prayers when an angel appears to her, announcing the forthcoming birth of a child:

> Suddenly, an angel of the Lord stood in front of her, saying, "Anna, Anna, the Lord God has heard your prayer. You will conceive and give birth and your child will be spoken of everywhere people live." And Anna said, "As the Lord God lives, whether I give birth to either a male or a female child, I will bring it as an offering to the Lord my God and it will be a servant to him all the days of its life." (*Gospel of James* 4:1–2)

The gospel then weaves an imaginative tale of Mary's unusual childhood. Anna keeps Mary in a bedroom that is kept entirely pure. Only the "pure daughters of the Hebrews" are allowed inside to play with her (6:4).

Keeping an earlier vow to the Lord, Anna presents her three-year-old daughter at the temple. All who beheld her find her to be special, and she is taken in to live in the temple. The gospel gives us an image of the little child Mary as she leaves her bedroom sanctuary to be received at the holy temple: "Let's call the pure women of the Hebrews. Let them take up lamps and light them so that the child will not turn back and her heart will never be led away from the temple of the Lord.' And they did these things until they went up to the temple of the Lord" (7:4–6).

Mary is received by the temple priest, who blesses her and "poured grace upon her." "And he set her down on the third step of the altar and the Lord God poured grace upon her" (7:9). The words of the priest provide another foreshadowing statement of Mary's future role as the mother of the Messiah, using language which parallels her song of praise, the Magnificat, featured in the gospel of Luke. "And the priest welcomed her. Kissing her, he blessed her and said, "The Lord God has magnified your name for all generations; through you the Lord will reveal deliverance to the children of Israel in the last days" (7:7–8).

Mary grows up in the temple until she reaches the age of twelve and the priest becomes concerned that her sexual maturity will defile the holy place (8:3–4). After praying about his predicament, God instructs him to have Hebrew widowers cast their lots for Mary's hand in marriage. The man who wins the honor is Joseph, an older man with sons from his previous marriage (8:7–8). This detail helps to explain the doctrine of Mary's perpetual virginity by explaining the appearances of Jesus' siblings in the canonical gospels.

Several years after this betrothal, sixteen-year-old Mary encounters an angel who tells her she will become pregnant with a savior (11:5–7). Once pregnant, she travels to her cousin Elizabeth's home, where she hides herself during the pregnancy (12:3). After six months, Joseph shows up at Elizabeth's doorstep to find Mary pregnant. He dramatically expresses his disdain, accusing her of being unchaste (13:1–5). However, an angel appears to Joseph in the night telling him that Mary was truthful and that the Holy Spirit conceived the baby (145–8). Joseph returns Mary to the temple and, seeing in her condition, the priest is horrified, instructing Mary to drink the "water of the Lord's wrath," and to go into the desert alone to reveal the truth surrounding her pregnancy.[4]

The ritual justifies Mary before the priest (James 16:5–8). She then goes into labor and Joseph seeks a Hebrew midwife to help deliver her baby in a cave. Initially, the fact that Joseph is not married to Mary scandalizes the midwife (18:1–2). However, when he shares the good news that the baby is the miraculously conceived savior, the midwife believes and rejoices. After the birth, the midwife tells a woman identified as Salome of what wonders she witnessed. Salome, skeptical, says that she will not believe such a thing unless she inserts her fingers into the new mother to test her virginity (19:7–19). Mary then undergoes a bizarre gynecological exam and, much like the well-known "doubting Thomas" in the Gospel of John, Salome is satisfied (20:1–4).

The conclusion to the *Gospel of James* feels rather hasty. Like the account given in the Gospel of Matthew, Mary and Joseph then travel to avoid Herod's command to execute all infant boys under the age of two, in an attempt to kill the Jewish Messiah (*Gospel of James* 22:1). The book then ends with the martyrdom of the prophet Zechariah, the husband of Elizabeth and father of John the Baptist (23:7–9).

The *Gospel of James* stands apart from the canonical gospels because of the careful details of Mary's birth, childhood, pregnancy, and delivery experience as mother of Jesus. The themes in the gospel highlight the blessedness and holiness of Mary in her own right. The author of the gospel wrote from a place of great devotion to Mary, denoting that she was already venerated in her own right at the time gospel was written. This gospel was in essence an apologetic work supporting the four dogmas of Roman

---

4. This passage mirrors the *Sotah* ritual, or the "Ritual of Bitter Water," found in Numbers 5:11–13.

Catholic Mariology: immaculate conception, mother of God, perpetual virginity, and assumption.

The account of Mary in the *Gospel of James* also shares many details with how she is memorialized in another religion: Islam. The *Gospel of James* sets the stage for introducing us to the great lady of Islam known as Maryam.

6

MARYAM

Mary in Islam

The figure of Mary is highly venerated not only in popular Muslim piety but within the Islamic sacred text (the Qur'an) as well as the tradition of the Prophet. However, reverence toward Mary—especially among Muslim women—exceeds the scholarly and textual exposition of her status within Islam.[1]

While most American Protestants know that Catholic beliefs about Mary are different than their own, they would be surprised by Bahar Davary's assessment of Mary's veneration in Islam. Islam is the only religion outside of the Christian tradition that honors Jesus as a spiritual figure. Islam, however, also honors his mother, Mary, in her own right. There are only eight *suras*[2] in the Qur'an named for individual people. *Maryam*, the nineteenth sura, is the only one named for a woman. In fact, Mary is mentioned by name more in the Qur'an than in the Bible.[3] Mary is also the only woman called by name in the Qur'an, and the only woman to never have been touched by sin.[4] Mary is considered

---

1. Davary, "Mary in Islam," 27.
2. *Sura* is the term for a chapter or section of the Qu'ran.
3. Ibid. Davary quotes Stowasser, *Women in the Qur'an*, 67.
4. Davary, "Mary in Islam," 29.

one of Islam's four examples of supreme womanhood.[5] She is "an exception-
ally pious woman with the highest spiritual rank among women."[6]

Details of Mary's life given in the Qur'an read closely to events found
in the New Testament gospels as well as the non-canonical *Gospel of James*,
all of which were written centuries before the Qur'an was believed to have
been revealed to Prophet Muhammad. Most scholars agree that the New
Testament gospels were written roughly between the years 70 and 110. The
Gnostic *Gospel of James* appeared around the year 145. The Qur'an appeared
centuries later, after the year 600. The Eastern and Coptic churches were
already flourishing at this time, so the convergence of these two religions in
the Middle East was a natural phenomenon.

Sura 19 is believed to have been written at a time when Muslims first
immigrated to Ethiopia. It is commonly accepted that the Muslim emigres
recited the book to the *Negus* (an Ethiopian royal title) to show themselves
as fellow believers in a monotheistic God, ensuring protection from enemy
attacks.[7] A more recent theory is that the book of *Maryam* was revealed
after the Prophet convened with a Christian delegation from the Saudi
Arabian city of Najran in 632. Muhammad used *Maryam* to seek common
ground in belief, while offering proof that Jesus was not the Son of God, in
an attempt to convert them to Islam.[8]

Before she appears in sura 19, Mary first appears in sura 3, named
Imran. In all, quranic references to Mary are found in suras 3, 4, 5, 19,
21, 23, and 66.[9] In the comprehensive article "The Virgin Mary in Islamic
Tradition and Commentary," authors Jane I. Smith and Yvonne Y. Haddad
divide the quranic Marian material into four categories: Mary's nativity,
Mary's retreat to the temple, the annunciation, and the Birth of Jesus. Let
us consider each topic.

MARY'S NATIVITY

An account of Mary's origin story is found in sura 3, *Imran*. Like the old,
barren wife of Zechariah, who miraculously gives birth to John the Baptist

---

5. Esposito, "What Everyone Needs to Know about Islam," 31.

6. Clooney, "Maryam in the Quran," line 30; Nasr, *Study Quran*, 763.

7. Stowasser, *Women in the Qur'an*, 72; Ibn Hishām and Ibn Ishāk, *Life of Muhammad*, 152.

8. Smith and Haddad, "Virgin Mary in Islam," 162.

9. Stowasser, *Women in the Qur'an*, 69.

in the New Testament, Mary's old and barren mother, Anna, finds herself pregnant.[10] She consecrates the child in her womb, and once Mary is born makes particular note that the child is a girl, and dedicates her daughter to God. Anna prays that her daughter will be protected from Satan, and will live a life of purity and goodness. To help ensure Mary's protection, her relative Zechariah is appointed as her guardian.

RETREAT INTO TEMPLE LIFE

As sura 3 continues, Zechariah is entrusted with Mary's care as she lives a life of piety in the temple. When caretaker Zechariah brings food to Mary's chamber, he finds that she has already been fed with food miraculously from God. Inspired by this miracle, Zechariah calls on God to give him a son even though he and his wife Elizabeth are old and infertile. Angels then prophesy the birth of John the Baptist, striking Zechariah mute for three days as a sign. This account of Zechariah's experience counterparts the similar story detailed in the Gospel of Luke 1. The same account is also repeated in sura 19.

THE ANNUNCIATION

> O Mary, indeed Allah has chosen you and purified you and chosen
> you above the women of the worlds. (sura 3:42)[11]

As Mary continues to live a pious temple life, sura 3 depicts Mary's visit from angels who tell of her chosen status and the gift of purity from Allah. The angels prophesy that she will bear a son named Jesus, who will be a Messiah to the children of Israel.[12] The prophecy comes to fruition in sura 19 when an angel in the form of a "well-formed" man visits Mary.[13] He tells her that she will miraculously conceive a son, who will be named Jesus and will be a Messiah. Mary questions the angel because she is a virgin. "How shall I have a boy when no man has touched me, nor have I been

10. Luke 1.

11. All quranic quotations are from Nasr's translation in *The Study Quran*.

12. Meaning "anointed one."

13. In tradition, the angel is considered to be Gabriel (Jibril); see Stowasser, *Women in the Qur'an*, 74.

unchaste?"[14] The angel answers: "'Thus [it will be]'; your Lord says, 'It is easy for Me, and We will make him a sign to the people and a mercy from Us. And it is a matter [already] decreed.'"[15]

Islamic tradition holds that the conception occurred when the angel blew the *Ruh*, or spirit of God, into Mary. Different embellishments have been added to the story over the centuries, detailing that he blew into her neckline, sleeve, or hem. In any case, the encounter left her miraculously pregnant with a son, fulfilling the prophecy.

THE BIRTH OF JESUS

After conceiving, Mary withdraws away from others. She eventually finds herself in labor all alone. "And the pains of childbirth drove her to the trunk of a palm tree. She said, 'Oh, I wish I had died before this and was in oblivion, forgotten.'"[16] Having compassion for her despair, God tells Mary not to worry and provides a stream of water for her to drink. God also instructs her to shake the tree she is sitting beneath, causing dates to fall which she can eat for nourishment and comfort.

After giving birth to a baby boy, Mary carries the child back to her home, where her family is taken aback and grieved by the sight of him; they understandably believe she has been unchaste and conceived the infant through natural means. In response, Mary simply points to the baby (19:29), who begins to speak like an adult: "[Jesus] said, 'Indeed, I am the servant of Allah. He has given me the Scripture and made me a prophet. And He has made me blessed wherever I am and has enjoined upon me prayer and *zakah* as long as I remain alive.'"[17] The baby Jesus goes on to prophesy further, effectively taking his place as a prophet while simultaneously denying his divinity or title of Son of God.

The Mary of the Qur'an experiences many similar events to those depicted in the Christian gospels. The following table provides a summary of the similarities and differences in the events of suras 3 and 19, the *Gospel of James*, and the New Testament canon.

---

14. Nasr, *Study Quran*, 19:20.
15. Ibid., 19:21–22.
16. Ibid., 19:23.
17. Ibid., 19:30–31.

Event	Gospel of James	Qur'an	New Testament
Mary's nativity	•	•	
Zechariah's son is foretold (John the Baptist).	•	•	•
Zechariah is struck mute for three days.	•	•	•
Wealthy Joachim (Mary's father) asks God for a child.	•		
Mary is cloistered in a bedroom at home.	•		
Mary retreats to live in the temple.	•	•	
Joseph is chosen to guard Mary.	•	•	
Mary is betrothed to Joseph.			•
The Angel Gabriel gives the annunciation; conception follows.	•	•	•
Mary gives birth alone beneath a tree; she is given water and dates from God.		•	
Mary gives birth in a cave as she travels with Joseph; he finds a Hebrew midwife.	•		
Mary gives birth in a manger in Bethlehem.			•

COMMON THEOLOGICAL THEMES

The Word Revealed

And the Word became flesh and lived among us, and we have seen his glory, the glory as of a Father's only Son, full of grace and truth. (John 1:14)

O Mary, truly God gives thee glad tidings of a Word from Him, whose name is the Messiah, Jesus son of Mary . . . (sura 3:45)

In Christian theology, Jesus is known as the Word of God incarnate. This concept most frequently identifies Jesus as *Logos*, the pre-Christian Greek term meaning both "word" and "reason."[18] When the Greek philosophers used the word *Logos*, it referred to the principle that creates and informs the universe. For Christians, the *Logos* became incarnate and entered the human world when born through Mary. For Muslims, the Word of God was delivered through a prophet, much like it was in the many prophets of the Jewish tradition. Muhammad, however, is considered a prophet above

18. Harris, *New Testament*, 490.

all prophets, having the holy text of Islam delivered directly to him, which he then gave to the world. According to Mary Joan Winn Leith, both Mary and Muhammad are human mediators, chosen to connect God to his people.[19] In each case, God could not deliver his Word to humanity without a human agent.

What then, does "Word" mean when used concerning Jesus in sura 3 of the Qur'an? In her work *Women in the Qur'an, Traditions, and Interpretation,* Barbara Freyer Stowasser considers the meaning of the term "Word" when interpreting Jesus' role and identification in the Qur'an. While several interpretations exist, Stowasser tells us that Muslim thinkers have largely considered the term "Word" to be metaphorical. This metaphor may express any of four possible theories:

1. God's creative power and an act of creation through Jesus;

2. The gospel or principle of Jesus' prophetic mission on earth;

3. Jesus symbolically referred to as "God's Word" to define his mission in the world;

4. God's message to Mary about the birth of Jesus.[20]

In any of these four suppositions, Jesus is not is divine. Because Jesus is not the divine *Logos,* the Mary of Islam is distinct from the Mary of Christianity because the Islamic version does not have the distinction of being named Theotokos, the God-Bearer. Muslim scripture and doctrine have carefully emphasized the mere humanity of Jesus, disputing his divinity.

An alternative and controversial opinion comes from Muslim scholar Martin Lings:

> According to the Koran, Jesus is both Messenger of God and also His Word which He cast unto Mary, and a Spirit from Him; and as it had been with the Word-made-flesh, so now analogously, it was through the Divine Presence in this world of the Word-made-book that Islam was a religion in the true sense of bond or link with the Hereafter. One of the functions of the Word-made-book, with a view to its primordial religion that Islam claimed to be/ was to reawaken in man his primeval sense of wonderment which, with the passage of time, had become dimmed or misdirected.[21]

19. Leith, "Mary and Muhammad," lines 30–33.

20. Stowasser, *Women in the Qur'an,* 76–77.

21. Lings, *Muhammad,* 68.

Though Lings receives some accusations of "Christianizing" or "perennial-ism" (perhaps influenced by his Anglicized roots), his claim that Jesus was Word-made-flesh in an Islamic context exhibits the way in which these two religions are able to be theologically intertwined.[22] As it seems, they are intertwined around Mary and her son, Jesus.

Purity and Virginity

As in all patriarchal religions, an emphasis on female sexual and physical purity exists in both Christianity and Islam. For Islam and Christianity, Mary is a paragon of female purity. Mary's purity is twofold: first, her purity of spirit as highly favored by God, demonstrated through her immaculate conception and chosen status to carry Jesus; second, by her physical virginity.

In the *Hadith*, Mary and Jesus are said to be the only two persons not touched by Satan at birth.[23] The concept of purity that is used for Mary, *tahara*, is a general virtue that all Muslims must possess as a prerequisite for worship. Bleeding, especially during menstruation, defiles a woman's purity. As a result, many exegetes have speculated about whether Mary menstruated, bled, after childbirth. Differing conclusions are reached by different authors of the *Hadith*. Stowasser teaches of the differing opinions between *Hadith*; some say Mary was physically like all women, while others say she was free from menstruation, which was the reason she was allowed to serve in the temple.[24]

Mary's purity is also exhibited through her virginity. In the Christian tradition, it is the most important part of her role in orthodoxy. Islamic tradition also makes it clear that no man had improper contact with Mary, as she was kept safe in the temple by Zechariah. Sura 19 tells that once she reached puberty she went behind a veil, which may have referred to a curtain that protected her from the male gaze.[25]

While a minority of Muslim scholars challenge the veracity of a virgin birth, most believe she was impregnated during her encounter with the

22. Haddad, "Critical Reading of Lings's Muhammad," 6. Haddad refers to Lings's "inept" treatment of Christian doctrines such as baptism, Eucharist, and assumption among others.

23. Smith and Haddad, "Virgin Mary in Islam," 172.

24. Stowasser, *Women in the Qur'an*, 78.

25. Nasr, *Study Quran*, Kindle ed., location 36711.

angel Gabriel. When Mary gave birth beneath a tree, she cried out that death would be a better fate. While an easy conclusion for those in postmodernity is that this was a garden-variety cry of extreme pain, some believe that her grief was not only caused by physical pain, but from shame over her condition and the fact that her family would believe she was unchaste, further supporting her purity of spirit and virginity.[26]

A New Eve—Fruit and Redemption

In the Christian tradition, Mary has been labeled the "new Eve," born without taint and canceling out the fall of women caused by Eve's sin of disobedience. In the Qur'an, however, the connection drawn between Mary and Eve is usually an apologetic support for the idea that Jesus was fully human, like God's first human creation, Adam. Muslim tradition also draws a parallel where Mary parallels Adam and Eve parallels Jesus. "Just as Eve was created from Adam without a woman, so was Jesus created from Mary without a man."[27] In this quadrilateral, one thing is certain: everyone involved is a human created by God.

Another obvious allusion to Eve is when Mary finds herself beneath the date tree, comforted by the fruit which God urges her to eat. According to Smith and Haddad, "Mary was given the assurance that she could eat what is fresh and appetizing and therefore be happy (with the implication that she need not fear the retribution of her relatives)."[28] While Smith and Haddad speculate that God gifts the fruit to alleviate fear of her relatives, it is also possible that God gives the fruit to symbolically forgive the sins of Eve. Eve's debt by fruit is now paid for by the obedience of Mary. The compassionate way in which God offers the fruit of this tree is the antithesis of his stern instruction not to eat of the fruit of the tree in the garden of Eden.

MARY THE PROPHET?

Because Mary is called by name in the Qur'an and has a sura named for her, it is natural to ask if Mary should be viewed as a Muslim prophet. A literalist school of Muslims known as the Zahirites have argued that Mary should

26. Ibid., location 36791.
27. Stowasser, *Women in the Qur'an*, 81.
28. Smith and Haddad, "Virgin Mary in Islam," 171.

indeed be counted among the prophets because an angel spoke directly to her. Another theologian, Ibn Hazim, makes the argument for Marian prophethood based on a verse calling her "a woman of truth" (sura 5:75), which is a turn of phrase used to describe the prophet Joseph.[29]

Sunni theology, however, calls any implication of Mary's prophet status to be heretical, using suras 12:109 and 16:43 as proof texts against female prophets.[30] Davary also makes the point that Sunni scholars generally hold that women cannot be prophets; Davary also cites Muhammad Abdel Haleem, who states that while only prophets are called by name in the Qur'an, Mary is the sole exception to the rule because of her role in the miraculous birth of the prophet Jesus.[31] Mary, it seems, causes a problem in the otherwise straightforward, patriarchal definition of a prophet.

Ladies of Suffering: Mary and Fatima

The well-known apparitions of Mary seen in the city of Fatima, Portugal, would likely be the first idea to come to the Christian mind when mentioning Mary and Fatima together. But long before those apparitions occurred, these two women shared a religious history in Islam. Like Mary, Fatima stands among the great ladies of Islam. Fatima was the daughter of the Prophet Muhammad and his wife Khadija. Islamic tradition teaches that Mary was one of the four women who miraculously aided Khadija during Fatima's birth, linking these two women from the very start.[32] From then on, Fatima and Mary have been specially connected, especially for Shi'a Muslims.

Like Mary, Fatima has been revered for her piety and as an ultimate expression of Muslim womanhood. Fatima and Mary are also both manifestations of the holy sufferer. Shi'a tradition correlates Hussein (the son of Fatima and grandson of the Prophet Muhammad) with Jesus based on their shared persecution and martyrdom.[33] Fatima has also been painted as a lady of sorrows based on her mourning for the Prophet as his only surviving

---

29. Stowasser, *Women in the Qur'an*, 77.

30. Ibid.

31. Davary, "Mary in Islam," 29; citing Haleem, *Understanding of the Quran*, 132.

32. Davary, "Mary in Islam," 31.

33. Ayoub, *Redemptive Suffering*, 35; Davary, "Mary in Islam," 32.

child. Despite the differences in their stories, Stowasser writes that for Shi'a, Mary and Fatima have virtually been melded into one figure.[34]

Just as she attended Fatima's birth, tradition places Mary at Fatima's side to console her suffering before death. Centuries after both women died, three children saw a series of Marian apparitions in Fatima, Portugal. Though the Fatima apparitions may have nothing to do with the great Fatima of Islam, one can't help but wonder about the reunification of these two pious women of different faiths once again.

Marian Bridges between the Muslim and Christian Worlds

"Devotion creates sentiments of friendship: it is a phenomenon open to everyone."[35] In the interfaith country of Lebanon, the date March 25 marks the Solemnity of the Annunciation, a day celebrated by both Muslims and Christians. Mary provides a bridge in interfaith spaces for those of different religious traditions to seek common ground.

Several mosques around the world are named for Mary. In the past, they have only existed in culturally Christian locations, like the Mary Mother of Jesus Mosque in Hoppers Crossing, Victoria, Australia; and Mosque Maryam, the Nation of Islam National Center, Chicago, Illinois. This changed in 2015 as a new Syrian mosque was named for Mary, a first in the Muslim world. Perhaps this was an action intended to serve as a statement of pluralism, celebrating the diversity in Syrian beliefs.[36]

Just as Mary served as a natural point of commonality with the pagan goddess worship that predated Christianity, Mary continues to serve as an important interfaith conduit. According to Father Miguel Angel Ayuso, who served as secretary of the eighth meeting of the Pontifical Council for Interreligious Dialogue, Mary is "a model for Muslims and Christians . . . a model of dialogue, teaching us to believe, not close ourselves up in certainties, but rather to remain open and available to others."[37]

---

34. Stowasser, *Women in the Qur'an*, 80.
35. "Virgin Mary in Islamic-Christian Dialogue," line 19.
36. "Mosque Dedicated to Virgin," lines 1–4.
37. "Virgin Mary in Islamic-Christian Dialogue," lines 40–41.

7

MARY'S SON

Christology, Virgin Birth, and Mary

Everything that the Church has said and says about the Mother is, in fact, at the service of Christ, in defense of his humanity and at the same time his divinity. Mariology is, in fact, Christology. Her dogmas are but the confirmation and bulwark of her Son's. Whenever Mary has been neglected, sooner or later Christ has also disappeared.[1]

The virgin birth of Jesus Christ is one of the rationally impossible beliefs that removes Christianity from the reach of modern, secular, post-Enlightenment thinking. For a woman to be impregnated by a supernatural spirit without the involvement of human male fertilization is, according to science and rational thought, most impossible. Because it is irrational and lacks historical proof, the virgin birth of Christ is just viewed as untrue. However, for millions of Christians the virgin birth is both real and sincerely believed. Because her role as Theotokos was vigorously defended and solidified by the patristic councils and later papal encyclicals, Mary firmly holds her place in the story of Jesus Christ. While some may argue that belief in the virgin birth may not be strictly necessary for a functional Christology, there is great theological value in its inclusion in Christian tradition and orthodoxy.

---

1. Zenit, "Messori and 'The Mary Hypothesis,'" lines 34–37.

This chapter will examine the denial of the virgin birth by modern theologians like those of the Quest for the historical Jesus. The next sections will consider several systematic theologians whose christological outlooks are compatible with Mary's role as a virgin. Then, I will give a brief analysis of the role of Mary in feminist Christology. Finally, I provide a personal narrative describing Mary's role in my understanding of the incarnation.

DENIAL OF THE VIRGIN BIRTH

After centuries of christological discourse following the early church councils, Christology was for the first time faced with the scrutiny of rationalism in the post-Enlightenment era. This Christology of modernity began with the groundbreaking Quest for the Historical Jesus, which first considered studying Jesus from a historical-scientific standpoint. This school of thought focused on what could be proven as factual by using the methods used by historians. Naturally, it follows that the virgin birth would come under fire from these theologians.

The First Quest for the Historical Jesus emerged in the nineteenth century when David Friedrich Strauss began to study Jesus Christ from a historical-critical standpoint, ultimately writing his controversial book *The Life of Jesus*. In this work, Strauss determined that the Bible is comprised of mythical material. However, this mythological character, according to Strauss, does not diminish the value of Scripture. This fact is particularly true because those who first created the narratives held mythology with great regard and value, and did not consider a mythical nature to invalidate a narrative.[2] For Strauss, it was Jewish eschatological belief coupled with information derived from first-hand encounters with Jesus that comprised the thrust behind the *mythus* of the biblical Jesus narrative.

After Strauss, the First Quest climaxed with the work of Albert Schweitzer. Schweitzer picked up Strauss's emphasis of Jewish eschatology as a defining framework for the Jesus narrative. He further added a theory that Jesus' story possesses no value outside of the original historical context in which Jesus lived, as well as emphasizing that any attempts to know who Jesus was as a historical personality are futile. First Quest theologians would not trouble themselves with a mythical phenomenon like the virgin birth. Because the virgin birth is a part of the mythology of the Jesus narrative,

2. Ibid.

there is no reason for these scholars to consider it beyond its place in the *mythus*.

The theological offspring of the historical quest scholars continued to espouse the idea that the virgin birth is mythical. One such successor is the well-known twenty-first-century "Jesus Seminar" scholar Marcus Borg. In his chapter in *The Meaning of the Birth Stories*, Borg details a hypothesis that the story of Jesus' virgin birth and the surrounding narratives were added to Matthew and Luke to emphasize the extraordinary birth of a remarkable child, and that the stories read like overtures to each gospel.[3] Dating Mark before and John after the birth narratives, Borg finds the fact that two separate and different gospels existed without any supporting birth story as lacking historical merit. Borg concludes that though they may not be "factual," that the stories are "true" as history metaphorized.[4] Of the virgin birth, Borg asserts that the story existed to affirm Jesus' divine origins.[5]

If the virgin birth is indeed merely mythical, Mary becomes nothing more than the mother of a notable spiritual leader. In other words, she becomes incidental if not wholly irrelevant to the story of Jesus of Nazareth. However, Quest historians are not the only christological scholars. Subsequent schools of thoughtfully support the role of Mary as Theotokos, a woman both worthy and necessary to form a solid, orthodox belief in Christ.

CHRIST PROCLAIMED: KÄHLER'S KERYGMATIC CHRISTOLOGY

Historical theology, like secular rationalism, has little use for the virgin birth. However, schools of systematic theology later emerged that eschewed the historical questers' strict adherence to historicity when doing theology. Systematic theology developed several different christological theories, which take differing points of departure when studying Christology. Systematic theologians pay careful attention to the *location* of the christological viewpoint; considering the sources of Christology as either proclaimed from the text of the gospel itself (*kerygma*), and from the belief of the worshippers (*pro me*) or as preached from the pulpit. Considering these three

3. Borg and Wright, *Meaning of Jesus*, 181.

4. Ibid., 182.

5. Ibid., 185.

main approaches, the proclamational theory of Christology is the most hospitable point of departure when considering the role of the virgin birth.

German theologian Martin Kähler began his christological discourse with a critique on the historical quests in his work *The So-Called Historical Jesus and the Historic Biblical Christ*. Kähler immediately states that the Quest for the Historical Jesus fails because there are no adequate historical, biographical materials available from which to know the Jesus of history.[6] Kähler, in turn, asks why it is that we seek to know Jesus. He concludes that as Christians we believe Jesus to be the Word of God, revealed to us through the incarnation.[7] Kähler emphasizes that the reader of the gospel does not seek an ordinary person of history, but sees someone who is the opposite of believers: a Savior.[8] Kähler concludes that the believer, in her reading of the biblical *kerygma*, or preaching, indeed seeks the "real Jesus." For Kähler , the real Jesus is not found in historical data but in the Christ who is preached.[9]

Kähler 's analysis makes a strong case for belief in the virgin birth of Jesus. Apart from the challenges of history and science, the virgin birth may sit securely within the proclamation of the Jesus Christ of faith. As Kähler points out, the believer seeks a Savior who is unlike the ordinary, sinful human. The biblical teachings of the miraculous birth of Jesus support the idea that he is indeed the mysterious incarnation of God revealed to us. Because this is not an ordinary man of history, and because the *kerygma* of the gospel preaches the virgin birth, there is no problem for Kähler in including the event as a part of the proclamation of Jesus Christ.

THE "FITTINGNESS" OF THE VIRGIN BIRTH

Twenty-first-century theologian Oliver D. Crisp considers a Christology without the virgin birth in his 2008 essay "On the 'Fittingness' of the Virgin Birth." Crisp presents a theoretical scenario in which there is no virgin birth associated with the incarnation, which he dubs the "NVB" version. In this exercise, Crisp assumes that the canonical account of Christ is entirely the same, except for the virgin birth. Christ still represents the Word become

---

6. Kähler, *So-Called Historical Jesus*, 48.

7. Ibid., 58.

8. Ibid., 59.

9. Ibid., 66.

flesh, but with different means as the catalyst.[10] In this scenario, Jesus was born as the naturally conceived son of Mary and Joseph, however, at the moment of natural conception, the Holy Spirit intervened by ensuring that the *ex nihlio* soul of Christ was without original sin and the Word of God assumed the soul.[11]

As Crisp examines his NVB hypothesis, he finds that the scenario does have a few problems. The first problematic conception is that Jesus might have two fathers, one human and one divine. However, he excuses this issue as no more damaging that the claim that Mary is mother of God, arguing that Joseph could be father of God in the same way, contributing to Christ's humanity just as Mary does.[12] Crisp also considers the moral problem of Jesus being born out of wedlock in an NVB hypothesis. This sinful act would not be an appropriate beginning for the sinless Jesus Christ. However, he goes on to say that his version of the NVB will assume marriage between Mary and Joseph before the conception of Jesus. Crisp concludes that his NVB account is ultimately compatible with both Chalcedonian dogma (without the virgin birth portion, of course). While the NVB theory satisfies Crisp theologically, he concludes that the virgin birth, apart from its existence in dogma and Scripture, is also a "fitting" means of incarnation.

Eleventh-century Catholic theologian Anselm of Canterbury wrote on the virgin birth, finding that virginal conception is fitting for four reasons: (1) God had not yet created a person via virginal conception, making the act remarkable; (2) since sin originated with Eve, it is fitting that salvation originated with Mary as a second Eve; (3) it allows for the redemption of womankind from Eve's sin, assuming that hope for women had been crushed by Eve; and (4) since Eve was created from a "virgin" Adam without human reproduction, it is fitting that Christ's humanity also came without human procreation.[13] Crisp agrees with Anselm's instincts, also stressing that the virgin birth wards off any doubts about adoptionism. Crisp also emphasizes that since the pre-existing *Logos* took human nature while remaining divine, this unique event is marked by the unique mode of conception and birth.[14]

10. Ibid., 208.
11. Ibid., 209.
12. Ibid., 210.
13. Ibid., 214.
14. Ibid., 216.

Crisp's focus on "fittingness" is arguably more convincing than Evans's argument for coherence. While the virgin birth is not rational, it is most definitely theologically fitting. The virgin birth's removal from christological doctrine is not helpful to the theology of the incarnation.

THE ROLE OF FEMINIST CHRISTOLOGY

Feminist theologian Elisabeth Schüssler Fiorenza provides a compelling methodology for creating a feminist Christology. Approaching Christ from what she calls "the *ekklesia* of women," Fiorenza's Christology would likely reject any Christian doctrine that sought to minimize the importance of Mary's role in the narrative.[15]

In her book *Jesus: Miriam's Child, Sophia's Prophet*, Schüssler Fiorenza emphasizes the importance of using feminist biblical interpretations when engaging in Christology from the viewpoint of the *ekklesia* of women.[16] Fiorenza's *ekklesia* of women is used to free theology from what she calls the "*kyriarchy*," the patriarchal structure inherent to theology and the church as we know it. To move away from the *kyriarchy*, Fiorenza instructs feminist scholars to form their theological ideas from within the women's liberation movement.[17] When feminist scholars position themselves within the liberation movement, they must also pay serious attention to the experiences of women when doing theological work. Considering the gospel accounts of Christ, the inclusion of Mary's birth narratives pays homage to her role as a mother and provides a purposeful female participation in Jesus' incarnation.

When we free Christology from the *kyriarchy* and read it from the position of the *ekklesia* of women, the elimination of the virgin birth takes away women's participation, erasing them from the honor of the divine event altogether. One may use Schüssler Fiorenza's description of the kyriarchy to argue that eliminating the virgin birth is indeed a *kyriarchal* act. The birth narratives, especially the one in the Gospel of Luke, give us a picture of Mary as a willing and faithful agent of God, who joyfully and bravely took on her role despite the reality that it would put her in danger. Unmarried, poor, and of an occupied people, her act provides an active female role in the incarnation, which would otherwise be diminished. If in

15. Schüssler Fiorenza, *Jesus: Miriam's Child.*

16. Ibid., 30.

17. Ibid., 208.

the alternative, Mary were a girl who was seduced or raped, her role would be that of an ordinary female under male domination and without sexual agency, whose baby was lucky enough to be chosen as the Savior. Through the annunciation, however, we learn that she is highly favored and full of grace, and is selected to participate in the creation of the Christ. Mary's favor and participation is an act that the *ekklesia* of women could most definitely support and celebrate

When viewing the virgin birth from a feminist perspective, we use the same proclamational Christology that Kähler gives us. The difference is that when the proclamation comes from the *ekklesia* of women, it is a proclamation from the female voices of the gospels. Because of this, feminist Christology should always defend and celebrate the virgin birth as a miraculous feminine role in the incarnation, despite all of the social oppression that human patriarchy has attempted to attach to the Virgin Mary herself.

MARIOLOGY IS CHRISTOLOGY

> Mariology cannot be developed from the naked fact, but only from the fact as it is understood in the hermeneutics of faith. In consequence, Mariology can never be purely Mariological. Rather, it stands within the totality of the basic Christ-Church structure and is the most concrete expression of its inner coherence.[18]

Like most theological topics, the question of the necessity of the virgin birth in Christology produces many different opinions. While some theologians like Schweitzer and Borg embrace a Christology that treats the virgin birth as mythical, others provide a framework where the virgin birth may be embraced and proclaimed as the origin of the Christ of faith. While Christians who doubt or reject the virginal birth as a necessary part of Christology are in sound theological company, there is also a refreshing body of theology that embraces the mystery of the virgin birth as the means of Jesus' incarnation. Though irrational and perhaps unnecessary, the virgin birth has found its way into the gospels, creeds, and hearts of millions of members of the church. Because of that, it is a rich and fitting part of the christological narrative; and within that narrative, Mary's role is indispensable.

18 Ratzinger, "Marian Doctrine and Piety," 156.

The incarnation is a christological concept that I have come to understand more deeply through the experience of motherhood. The final section of this chapter shares my personal experience with motherhood and my appreciation for Mary's part in the incarnational aspect of Christology.

THE INCARNATION AND MOTHERHOOD

One cold Cleveland night, I walked up the aisle of a church, my husband by my side. It was the warm and glowing liturgical season of Advent, and we were chosen to light the third candle of Advent: the merry candle. The distinctively pink candle, among purple ones, some refer to as the joy candle or the love candle. For me, with my growing belly traveling the aisle in front of me, I was acutely aware of the reason we were chosen for the honor. It was also the first time I had given any real religious thought to Mary.

The season of Advent is the one time that Mary may make an appearance in the Protestant church. It is the time when our scriptural reading turns to Mary's big scene, the miraculous conception and birth of the Savior. As the nativity figures are set up in the sanctuary, and a girl from the youth group dons a blue robe for the Christmas pageant, we are treated to the only representation of Mary many Protestants know. After lighting that rose-colored candle, my eyes were opened to the warm, life-giving glow that, to me, represents Mary.

I had been married only a year when I discovered I was pregnant with my first (and only) child. Married on my twenty-sixth birthday, my husband and I came to the mutual decision to wait a few years before starting a family. I was young and unconcerned with my maternal clock and wanted to spend time traveling, saving money, and building a solid marriage. As it often does for those who have careful plans, the time line did not take the shape we imagined. I was married, well educated, and economically secure; but these things did not prevent me from experiencing the fears and anxieties that come with being pregnant for the first time. From the physical stresses to the sleepless nights spent wondering if I was ready to care for a tiny human life, the entire season of pregnancy was more than a bit frightening. Was I up to this job?

Then I was sent to light a joyful pink candle while simultaneously thinking of Mary's situation. Young, unmarried, betrothed and a virgin, Mary was infinitely more vulnerable when she found herself pregnant than I, as a middle-class, twenty-first-century American woman, was. I knew where my baby came from and why, and my husband was ready and willing to share the experience at my side. Mary, however, received an unbelievable visit from an angel announcing the incomparable charge she was given: mothering the Messiah.

Pregnancy was admittedly not easy for me. I suffered from morning sickness, unhealthy weight gain, anxiety, and a host of other challenges. But when I was feeling small, scared, or unprepared, I thought about Mary. She was likely a young teenager, living in a society where much was insecure for a girl of her marginalized ethnicity and low social class. Beyond that, she was a girl in a society where the perception of her virtue, consensual or otherwise, was tethered to her economic, social, and physical security. Her act of accepting her pregnancy with bravery inspired me.

As years pass and I raise my child, I still think of Mary. Now, however, I reflect on the way she nursed, loved, and cared for Jesus. Like my daughter, Jesus was a tiny, vulnerable, fully human baby who needed his mother to survive. The act of mothering, with all of its unglamorous aspects, is an intensely human experience. Feeding, bathing, and nursing sickness are the actions of a human parent. Through these encounters, I gained the ability to see Jesus as a genuine person, not an intangible spirit. I also gained a deeper appreciation for his sacrifice on the cross. Jesus experienced real agony as Mary watched. He suffered real emotional anguish, as did his mother. Blood and tears are the stuff of life; God chose to become incarnate and embrace humanity in the most authentic way possible. Jesus, fully God and fully human, finally made sense to me.

The prolific philosopher Soren Kierkegaard described full self-giving through a parable that is often used as a metaphor for the incarnation. In the parable, a mighty king desperately loves a humble maiden. It is only through truly changing his identity and taking on the life of a low-born man that he can share the love he desired.[19] Kierkegaard writes: "But as love is the motive so love must also be the end; for it would be a contradiction for the God to have a motive and an end which did not correspond. His love is a love of the learner, and his aim is to win him. For it is only in love that the unequal can be made equal, and it is only in equality or unity that an understanding can be effected . . ."[20] Through the incarnation, God chose to renounce his supremacy through becoming the human Christ. This act of love for humankind would not be authentic without experiencing every

19. Kierkegaard, *Parables*, 40.
20. Ibid., 41–42.

detail of being human. Genuine human life is impossible without being born of a woman. Enter Mary, an indispensable presence in the story of the incarnation.

8

A FEMINIST CRITIQUE OF MARY

Steeped in a tradition of patriarchy beginning with the Jewish faith and ending with the organized Christian church, it is no surprise that many feminists regard Christianity as hostile territory for women. Simone de Beauvoir's 1949 *The Second Sex* is considered an important text in the development of twentieth-century feminist theory. In the book, de Beauvoir gives the Christian religion harsh criticism.[1] Within this criticism, the Virgin Mary serves as a symbol of this oppression, viewing her as a symbol of second-class female citizenship and an unobtainable and highly limiting ideal for women. With the advent of feminist theology, the Marian tradition continued to be a place of tension for feminist scholars. While more radical voices sought to condemn Mariology as irredeemable, others potential for a sound feminist Mariology.

While some male scholars took on the task of giving Mariology a critical analysis that considered feminist concepts, the rise of influential women scholars provided a much-needed diagnosis of the way Mariology effects the women in the church. Predictably, Roman Catholic scholars have produced the body of feminist mariological work, demonstrating the importance of personal experience in any scholarship that seeks to amplify marginalized voices. Just as the church has spent centuries developing the patriarchal Mariology that these scholars use as a starting point, notable feminist theologians have each carefully considered their vision for a feminist look at Mary. Each scholar arrived at different conclusions. This chapter

1. Beauvoir, *Second Sex*, 133.

will review the work of five of these scholars, providing a broad overview of the state of feminist Mariology.

MARY DALY

The earliest and most radical thinker, Mary Daly, was a Catholic scholar whose earlier works sought justice and reform within the church, arguing that equality was possible within the scope of organized religion, as discussed in her 1968 book *The Church and the Second Sex*. However, Daly is best known for her later works, which gave a much more radical feminist philosophy and fatalistic view of women's potential for equality within the church.

In her 1973 work *Beyond God the Father: Toward a Philosophy of Women's Liberation*, Daly stresses that her work does not attempt to in any way fix the patriarchal Mariology of the past, but seeks to show how Marian symbolism has served as a "two-edged sword" for the women of the church.[2] She criticizes the way that Mary is only relationally significant; that is, without Christ she does not matter.[3] Daly then goes on to analyze the Marian doctrines formally adopted in modernity: the immaculate conception and the assumption.

For Daly, the immaculate conception was originally conceived to reinforce the idea of the inherent evil of the feminine, redeeming the fallen Eve by being sanctified. Daly offers an alternative view of the doctrine that considers the immaculate conception as representative of the mother goddess symbol that predates Christianity.[4]

The assumption also provides hope for a picture of Mary without patriarchal context. In the assumption, Daly sees a prophetic nature in Mary.[5] Carl Jung found feminist value in the assumption by focusing on Mary's rising into a place of prestige, considering her a "fourth person" of the Trinity.[6] While this theory has some value, Daly argues that it falls short, both because the church has not accepted it and because the pope who instituted the assumption as dogma was decidedly working within a patriarchal framework. Daly concludes that the "extreme dichotomy" of the

2. Daly, *Beyond God the Father*, 83.
3. Ibid., 84.
4. Ibid., 86.
5. Ibid., 87.
6. Ibid., 89.

prophetic symbolism of Mary and the social degradation of women by the Catholic Church may be viewed as a "compensation mechanism"[7]; mainly that the church and its all-male, celibate priesthood use and manipulate Mary to symbolically give a needed feminine energy to the church while maintaining full patriarchal control.[8]

By 1978 Daly's view of Mary moved even further to the theological left. In *Gyn/Ecology: The Metaethics of Radical Feminism*, Daly emphatically rejects the Mary of Scripture, including the virgin birth, as wholly mythologized. Daly also emphasizes the fact that Mary has no meaningful role in the events of the annunciation, conception, and birth of Jesus. For Daly, Mary does nothing. She takes no self-determined steps to add any value to the christological story. She simply served as a walking womb. Daly rejects the view that Mary may be lauded as one who committed an act of parthenogenesis, one whose egg reproduces without male fertilization.[9] Daly takes Mary's inaction even further by naming her as a "total rape victim," experiencing a "mind/spirit" rape that eliminated the need for physical rape.[10]

ROSEMARY RADFORD RUETHER

Rosemary Radford Ruether is a more moderate contemporary of Mary Daly. Radford Ruether's work is heavily influenced by a liberation theology that views liberation for "the least of them" as the key component to creating feminist theology. Regarding Mary, Radford Ruether takes what Elisabeth Schüssler Fiorenza would later call an "ideal-typical" view of Mariology.[11] In her 1977 book *Mary: The Feminine Face of the Church* and also her later work *Sexism and God-Talk*, Mary symbolizes the whole of liberated humanity; those who experience various marginalized identities serve as the basis for a liberation Mariology. Radford Ruether writes that "Mary as Church represents God's 'preferential option for the poor,'" a term she borrows from Latin American liberation theology.[12]

---

7. Ibid., 89.
8. Ibid., 89–90.
9. Daly, *Gyn/Ecology*, 83.
10. Ibid., 83–84.
11. Schüssler Fiorenza, *Jesus: Miriam's Child*, 188–89.
12. Ruether, *Sexism and God-Talk*, 157.

Radford Ruether places her argument squarely within the so-called liberation gospel of Luke, known for a focus on particularly marginalized peoples, especially those with intersecting marginalized identities.[13] The emphasis on "the least" coupled with the notion that Mary represents the feminized church (an idea that is well-established within the patriarchal church) makes Radford Ruether's feminist Mariology moderate and workable within the mainstream church.[14] This was particularly true because the liberation theologians of Latin America flourished during this period, thus giving her male-centric voices to lend support to her viewpoint. Nonetheless, Radford Ruether gives readers a feminist Mariology that is likely more relatable for church women than Mary Daly's radical rejectionism.

ELIZABETH JOHNSON

Scholar Elizabeth Johnson's twenty-first century Mariology furthers the quest for a workable feminist Mariology within the church. Her 2006 book *Truly Our Sister: A Theology of Mary in the Communion of Saints* paints a portrait of Mary as both prophet and friend. Johnson lays out a comprehensive overview of what she calls "androcentric Mariology," then looks for precedents for her own feminist Mariology. For Johnson, the use of women's voices is key to developing a satisfying feminist view of Mary, replacing voices of patriarchy and kyriarchy with the voices of a pluralistic group of women.

Johnson values Pope Paul VI's four mariological guidelines as a jumping off point for her thought. Paul VI's Mariology must be: (1) biblical, (2) liturgical, (3) ecumenical, and (4) anthropological. Paying careful attention to the biblical and ecumenical aspects, Johnson uses the Mary of Scripture to mosaic an image of Mary who encapsulates the full history and experiences of women.[15]

Johnson also focuses on Mary as a "woman of Spirit."[16] Johnson views the Mary of Scripture as one who lived following the Holy Spirit, or the feminine "Spirit-Sophia," which represents divine wisdom. Like Radford Ruether, Johnson also notes Mary's station as "the least," especially in Luke's gospel, where she sings her liberation song, the Magnificat. In conclusion,

13. Ibid., 152–57.
14. Ibid.
15. Johnson, *Truly Our Sister*, 209.
16. Ibid., 263.

Johnson names Mary as both prophet and companion. A woman of Spirit, her prophecy is the raising of her voice against injustice on God's behalf.[17] A companion, she also shows us the holiness of the ordinary women, especially marginalized women. Through her life in the Spirit, Mary serves as a friend to those in the communion of saints.

MARY C. GRAY

Scholar Mary C. Gray uses both liberation theology and process theology to develop her feminist Mariology. Gray's concern with mainstream Mariology is based on Vatican II's Marian doctrine as expressed in *Lumen Gentium*. The ecumenical focus of the Vatican council resulted in a highly "relational" Mariology, meaning that Mary's value exists solely in relationship with her son, Jesus Christ. For Gray, "relational language" cannot provide the basis for a feminist Mariology.[18] Gray sees other problems with patriarchal Mariology, such as the impossibility of a permanent state of virginity for ordinary mothers, as well as the sexual problem of designating the female sex act as one that is solely for procreation and the vocation of motherhood. Gray also notes that Mary's "perfect womanhood" stifles the self-determination of women.[19]

Instead of keeping these problematic concepts of Mary, Gray urges us to read Mary within the context of all of the other women of the Bible, especially subversive figures such as Rahab and Tamar.[20] Gray also notes the importance of removing and reclaiming motherhood from the confines of the patriarchy. Instead, the focus should be fixed on the creative nature of the act of birthing.[21] Finally Gray looks to Mary's qualities as redeemer in her own right. Gray writes, "if we can see the redemptive process, not simply as Cross/Resurrection, but as Creation/Incarnation/ Redemption/ New Jerusalem—all as unified process, then we can see Mary both as symbolizing redeemed creation, and as summoning women to contribute both to our own and to the world's redemption."[22]

17. Ibid., 307.
18. Gray, "Reclaiming Mary," 336.
19. Ibid.
20. Ibid., 337.
21. Ibid., 338.
22. Ibid., 340.

ELISABETH SCHÜSSLER FIORENZA

Elisabeth Schüssler Fiorenza's feminist christological work *Jesus: Miriam's Child, Sophia's Prophet* stays closely locked in step with Mary throughout her analysis. In the book's final chapter, "In Her Image and Likeness," Fiorenza takes on Mariology directly, providing a feminist Mariology to accompany her Christology. For Fiorenza, Mary has been "mythologized beyond recognition," requiring us to fully deconstruct the Marian cult as well as its history and images.[23] For Fiorenza, existing Mariology is inherently patriarchal, or what she refers to as "malestream."[24] Her goal is to treat feminist Marian thought in a way that will not enlarge the marginalization of women the way that previous thought has done.

Fiorenza notes that previous feminist Mariology has concentrated on dismantling the cult of Mary rather than taking a "sociohistorical approach."[25] She also argues that substituting a feminist mythology also runs the risk of encountering the existing "kyriarchal limitations" in the church.[26] With these constraints in mind, she gives us the four methods of feminist Mariology that remain problematic:

1. a Reformation approach, that entails cutting back on Marian excess with a focus on her history;

2. an ideal-typical approach, which looks to Mary as representative of the modern church and humanity;

3. a doctrinal-mythologizing approach, which places correlations between Mary and the mythology of a "divine mother goddess" into the dogma; and finally,

4. a cultic-spiritual approach, in which Mary is no longer an ordinary human, but a feminine representation of God.[27]

In response, Fiorenza provides four strategies that she believes provide a workable feminist Mariology. The Latin terms she gives these strategies are *via negativa, via affirmativa, via eminentia,* and *via practica.*[28]

---

23. Schüssler Fiorenza, *Jesus: Miriam's Child,* 180.
24. Ibid., 181.
25. Ibid., 182.
26. Ibid., 183
27. Ibid., 184–92.
28. Ibid., 198–99.

1. *Via negative.* This idea is based on the fact that no human language can adequately speak about the Divine. As mere humans, we cannot with authority say what God is; however, can say what God is *not*, meaning not a man, woman, king, queen, father, or mother. The same idea applies to Marian language; seeking to identify Mary with a largely generalized "eternal feminine" does not work.

2. *Via affirmative.* Conversely, we can positively ascribe the positive characteristics that we know God possesses; mainly, a good and loving God of liberation who desires well-being for God's creation. Importantly, everyone of any identity is the image of God. Fiorenza applies the same standard to Mary, noting that she is all identities, making diverse human representations of Mary crucial. This approach returns Mary to the "ekklesia of women."

3. *Via ementia.* This approach retains the rich tradition of Marian symbols and metaphors that already exist in the cult of Mary, but with a focus on reconstructing and reintegrating them into God language in a way that would lead to an effective demythologization of both Jesus and Mary.

4. *Via practica.* This final approach borrows God language and Marian symbolism from the solidarity of the anti-patriarchal liberation movement. Here Mary represents the least of us and the need for their liberation.

After employing the philosophy she uses for a useful feminist Mariology, Fiorenza discusses the visitation of Mary with Elizabeth in the context of the sexual violence against women in occupied territories. While biblical literalists accept the visitation and virginal conception as orthodoxy, others who read the Bible in an allegorical manner believe that Mary was either sexually active with Joseph or raped by a Roman soldier. Mary was a vulnerable young girl in an occupied territory. Like other women and girls who have experienced military and colonial occupation, it is possible that Mary was the victim of ethnically motivated sexual violence. Mary's vulnerability in her pregnant state may be interpolated from the fact that she took a long and arduous journey through the hill country to seek the company and counsel of a female relative outside of her immediate family.[29]

29. Ibid., 200–202.

Some feminist theologians have accepted the visitation as representative of Mary's independence from a man. Fiorenza quotes Sojourner Truth, who famously said, "Where did your Christ come from? From God and a woman. Man had nothing to do with him."[30] However, Fiorenza points out that those who do not believe the orthodox view of the visitation may find great value in the "dangerous memory" of Mary as a young, unwed mother, frightened and vulnerable.[31] Akin to the other subversive, socio-sexually marginalized women in the Gospel of Matthew's genealogy of Jesus—Tamar, Rahab, Bathsheba, and Ruth—Mary was an example of "the other," pregnant under unromantic and dangerous circumstances. It was from here that she birthed the Christian tradition into existence.

> In the center of the Christian story stands not the lovely "white lady" of artistic and popular imagination, kneeling in adoration before her son. Rather it is the young pregnant woman, living in occupied territory and struggling against victimization and for survival and dignity. It is she who holds out the offer of untold possibilities for a different Christology and theology.[32]

Fiorenza's Mariology cuts to the heart of her experience as a woman on the fringes, a woman charged with pregnancy before her time and without society's approval. This "dangerous memory" of Mary serves as a worthy feminist inspiration point for creating a womanist Mariology.[33]

30. Ibid., 204.
31. Ibid., 205.
32. Ibid., 206.
33. Ibid., 205.

PART 3

A WOMANIST MARIOLOGY

9

STABAT MATER DOLOROSA
Black Mothers, Slain Children

At the Cross her station keeping,
stood the mournful Mother weeping,
close to her Son to the last.[1]

M ary's presence at the crucifixion is a sorrowful part of the passion narrative.[2] As Jesus hung on the cross in agony, we imagine
that Mary stood nearby, weeping mournfully. The *Stabat Mater*
is a lyrical text that several composers like Antonin Dvorak and Giovanni
Battista Pergolesi have set to music. A literal definition of the title *Stabat
Mater Dolorosa* is "standing mother painful."[3] The lyrics of the *Stabat Mater*
describe a mourning Mary, experiencing her son's pain on the cross. In
the tradition of European art and music, Mary is a figure receiving great
sympathy and is revered for her role as the mother of Jesus.

Mary's son Jesus experienced the most famous state-initiated execu-
tion of all time. However, Mary's story is entirely unique. For believers,
her son Jesus rose from the dead and ascended into heaven. The Apostle's

1. In Caswall, *Lyra Catholica*, 138.

2. The Gospel of John is the only gospel to place Mary at the cross specifically.

3. Translation from "William Whitaker's Words," http://archives.nd.edu/words.
html.

79

Creed tells believers that Jesus sits at the right hand of the Father, and Mary has earned titles like Theotokos or Queen of Heaven. Because of their roles in the foundation of Christianity, both Jesus and Mary have left an indelible legacy behind them.

But what about the Black mothers who have lost their children at the hands of the state through police violence? What about the mothers who have lost their children at the hands of racially motivated vigilantes? None of these children received a trial before their death, and their deaths were in vain. The grieving mothers of victims of racially charged shootings receive no societal adoration. In fact, they often experience blame and vilification for their own children's deaths. No one has written a lyrical and poignant *Stabat Mater Dolorosa* for the mothers of these slain children.

In this chapter, we consider the violent deaths of several Black children and the ways society treats their mothers. In addition to several highly publicized killings, the chapter concludes with anecdotes of several incidents I encountered during my time living in Cleveland, Ohio.[4] Through these experiences, we embark on our quest to create a womanist Mariology.

MAMIE AND EMMETT

The well-known story of the murder of Emmett Till haunts history to this day. Fourteen-year-old Emmett was the only son of Mamie Till. Mamie was a devout member of the Pentecostal Church of God in Christ. She was known as a strict, devoted mother. When she decided to visit her family in Nebraska during the summer of 1955, she never imagined that her son would meet such a tragic fate while visiting his cousins in Mississippi.[5]

Emmett was accused of whistling at a twenty-one-year-old married white woman named Carolyn Bryant. As a result, he was abducted by Bryant's husband and his half-brother and was brutalized, murdered, and mutilated. Mamie was obviously devastated when she learned of the killing. "When I began to make the announcement that Emmett had been found and how he was found, the whole house began to scream and to cry. And

---

4. Womanist theology is heavily influenced by the experiences of Black women, which is discussed in chapter 10 of this volume. For this reason, I share my relevant personal experiences.

5. "Murder of Emmett Till: Timeline," "Murder of Emmett Till: People and Events – Mamie Till Mobley."

that's when I realized that this was a load that I was going to have to carry. I wouldn't get any help carrying this load."[6]

In Mamie's grief, she decided to present her son's body in an open casket for all to see the state of his body and the viciousness of his murder. Upwards of fifty thousand people attended Emmett's Chicago funeral. His mutilated body was on display, shocking the public with its appearance and smell.[7]

Unfortunately, Mamie saw no justice served for her son's death, as an entirely white male jury acquitted both defendants after only sixty-seven minutes of deliberation.[8] The acquittal, however, was not rendered before Mamie Till and Black motherhood were put on trial. While the prosecutor argued that Black women "too" loved their children and recognized their bodies with a natural maternal sense, the defense argued that Mrs. Till could not and did not know if the body was indeed her son's.[9] She was also placed on trial herself, being asked to prove that she had been a good mother who raised Emmett "correctly." In fact, one Southern white woman told the media that Mrs. Till was herself to blame for allowing Emmett to visit Mississippi: "She should have had better sense than to let such a child come here."[10] After the acquittal, one juror questioned Mamie's veracity and love for her son by saying, "if she had tried a little harder . . . she might have got out a tear."[11]

Mamie Till was not the first nor the last Black mother to see her child suffer an unjust death. Mamie and many others devoted their lives to protecting the lives of Black people. Sadly, in the twenty-first century, the age of Black Lives Matter has brought light to several cases where Black children were killed and assailants went unpunished.[12]

---

6. PBS, "Mamie Till Mobley."

7. Ibid.

8. Feldstein, "I Wanted the Whole World to See," 264.

9. Ibid., 280.

10. Ibid., 276.

11. Ibid., 281.

12. Black Lives Matter is a slogan and social justice movement working against racially motivated violence toward Black people.

TRAYVON AND SYBRINA

In February 2012, Trayvon Martin was shot and killed by a private citizen, George Zimmerman. Trayvon was an unarmed seventeen-year-old walking down a public sidewalk when he was pursued by George Zimmerman, an adult who suspected Martin of criminal wrongdoing. After a confrontation, Zimmerman shot and killed Trayvon Martin. Zimmerman was not immediately charged with homicide because his account was accepted as fact by the sheriff, who believed that Florida's "Stand Your Ground" law applied to the situation.[13] George Zimmerman was later charged with second-degree murder and manslaughter by a special prosecutor, but was acquitted on all counts by a Florida jury in 2013.[14]

Trayvon's mother, Sybrina, said this about the verdict: "'When I heard the verdict, I kind of understand the disconnect . . . Maybe they (jurors) didn't see Trayvon as their son. They didn't see Trayvon as a teenager. They didn't see Trayvon as just a human being that was minding his own business.'"[15]

Trayvon was a teenage Black boy killed more than fifty years after Emmett Till. However, the problem of slaying Black children is a problem today just as it was in the Jim Crow–era South. While the narrative usually focuses on young Black men and teens, Black girls also face the dangers of dying by homicide and lack of justice.

THE DEATH OF AIYANA JONES

At 12:40 a.m. on May 16, 2010, the Detroit Police Department Special Response Team raided an apartment on the east side of Detroit. During the raid, seven-year-old Aiyana Jones was shot and killed while sleeping on the couch.[16]

Detroit police were acting on a warrant to search the premises where Aiyana was sleeping. They used a flash grenade to distract and stun the apartment's occupants, then, led by Officer Joseph Weekley, proceeded to

---

13. Florida's "Stand Your Ground" law is an affirmative defense that may be raised if a person uses deadly force to defend themselves. See Peralta, "Martin Puts Stand Your Ground in Spotlight."

14. Alvarez and Buckley, "Zimmerman Acquitted."

15. Ford and Carter, "Justice System Didn't Work for Us," lines 28–31.

16. Schaeffer, "Detroit Police Outline Final Moments."

raid the apartment in full riot gear. Officer Weekley reports that Aiyana's grandmother, Mertilla Jones, reached for his gun, which he says caused his gun to fire, killing Aiyana. Mertilla Jones was arrested based on the officer's statement, but no gunpowder or fingerprint evidence was found to corroborate the officer's story. Mertilla insists that she reached for her granddaughter in the midst of the raid, not for the officer or his weapon.[17]

The legal aftermath of Aiyana's death was irregular from beginning to end. The first trial of Officer Weekley ended in a mistrial in June of 2013. His next trial also had procedural issues. The judge put the trial on a temporary hold after both Mertilla and Aiyana's mother, Dominika, had emotional outbursts on the witness stand. Mertilla was eventually removed from the courtroom for screaming and was not allowed to return. The presiding judge stated that if any of Aiyana's relatives had future outbursts on the witness stand, he would declare a mistrial.[18]

On October 3, the judge dismissed the involuntary manslaughter charge against Weekley. On October 10, the judge declared second a mistrial due to jury deadlock.[19] Finally, on January 28, 2015, county prosecutor Kym Worthy dismissed the last remaining charge against Weekley: a misdemeanor for carelessly discharging a firearm causing death. Weekley will not have a third trial.[20] No one will be held legally culpable for Aiyana's death.

Dominika received no justice for the death of her young daughter. Grandmother Mertilla was publicly chastised for her emotional breakdown while recalling the night she saw her granddaughter shot dead. Aiyana was a little girl who was shot while she slept in her family home. The world will likely forget all three of them altogether. There will be no *Stabat Mater Dolorosa* composed for Dominika, and no requiem for Aiyana.

TAMIR AND SAMARIA

Tamir Rice was a twelve-year-old Cleveland boy who was seen playing with a toy gun in a neighborhood park. Someone called the police, reporting that an individual was pointing a gun at people in the park, located outside

17. Gutherie and Hunter, "Slain Girl's Family Alleges Police Cover-Up"; "Grandmother's Fingerprints, DNA Not Found."

18. Anderson, "Manslaughter Charge Dismissed."

19. "Second Mistrial Declared."

20. "Prosecutor: No Third Trial."

of a recreation center. The caller described a "male Black sitting on a swing and pointing a gun at people" and later said during the dispatch call that the gun was "probably fake."[21] When two Cleveland officers arrived on the scene, they shot Tamir within seconds. During the chaos, the police officers also tackled Tamir's fourteen-year-old sister, Tajai, as she was tried to rush to Tamir after his shooting.[22] The entire encounter was captured on surveillance video.

On December 28, 2015, a Cuyahoga County grand jury declined to indict the officers involved in the shooting. A mere three days after Christmas, Samaria Rice learned that there would be no one held accountable for her son's death. She reportedly wept so much she could barely speak.[23] The Rice family released this statement:

> Prosecutor McGinty deliberately sabotaged the case, never advocating for my son, and acting instead like the police officers' defense attorney. In a time in which a non-indictment for two police officers who have killed an unarmed black child is business as usual, we mourn for Tamir, and for all of the black people who have been killed by the police without justice. In our view, this process demonstrates that race is still an extremely troubling and serious problem in our country and the criminal-justice system.[24]

Public Responses to Tamir's Death

Perhaps predictably, instead of sympathy for Tamir's death and justice for her family, Samaria Rice was met with vitriol: "Raise your kids not to play with fake guns you stupid bitch."[25] These are the words of a Cleveland police officer named Matthew Cicero. He posted this statement about Samaria on social media shortly after the grand jury opted not to indict the officers who shot Tamir.[26]

It is hard to imagine a more disrespectful statement toward a mother who lost a young child. However, this vicious statement is not the only criticism Samaria has received. From the time of Tamir's shooting, the media

21 Izadi and Holley, "Video: Officer Shooting 12-Year-Old."

22. Ferrise, "Rice's Sister: Police Officer 'Attacked Me.'"

23. Golston, "Attorney: Mother of Tamir Rice Wept."

24. Ibid.

25. Buduson, "Office Under Investigation."

26. Ibid.

and the public did not treat Samaria Rice as a grieving mother whose innocent son was killed. In a reprisal of the treatment Mamie Till received, many looked for reasons to blame Samaria for her son's death, or at the very least to make her unworthy of our sympathy.

Samaria's criminal record was immediately thrust into the media spotlight. She has been harshly questioned as an adequate mother, as shown by the statement of the Cleveland police officer. Cuyahoga County prosecutor Timothy McGinty even made a disturbing statement that he thought that the Rice family was pursuing a case against the police officers to seek financial gain.[27] Also, the media repeatedly reported that Tamir was 5'7", making the excuse that could have looked like an adult in the eyes of the officers. Much of the public seemed to desire to justify Tamir's death and diminish Samaria's pain.

Samaria Rice is a grieving mother. Her blameless son died at the hands of the law. But unlike Mary, there will be no *Stabat Mater Dolorosa* written for her. We won't soon see Samaria and Tamir sculpted into a Pietà.

One of the most common depictions of Mary in visual art is what is known as the Pietà. Pietà translates from Italian as "lamentation." In paintings and sculptures of the Pietà, Mary laments while cradling Jesus' battered body. Samaria was not able to hold her son's body at the scene of his death. When his sister tried to be by his side, she was tackled to the ground by adult men.

Mary mourned her son as any mother would. She was at the cross when he died, and she was at the tomb when he was resurrected three days later. Jesus defeated death, but Samaria's son will not live again. As an ordinary boy in an ordinary world, Tamir's earthly life ended with a bullet on Cleveland pavement.

THE BLACK MOTHERS OF CLEVELAND

While Samaria Rice's story has made headlines, many Cleveland-area families have experienced police misconduct. Those that live to tell the tale could have easily ended up with the same fate as Tamir. Though these problems exist elsewhere, the Black mothers of Cleveland live in fear for their children, especially their sons.

The city of Cleveland Heights is a suburb, but it is adjacent to both Cleveland and the notorious East Cleveland, a city known for its high crime

27. Reid, "Lawyer Blasts Prosecutor's Remarks."

rate and extreme poverty. Cleveland Heights works hard to preserve the town's reputation for the college students and young professionals who enjoy living near the city's eclectic shopping, ethnic eateries, and sports bars. To accomplish this, the municipality has a remarkable police presence, known for cruising the streets, frequently ticketing for minor traffic infractions and questioning anyone on the street whom they deem suspicious. Their suspicion meter was especially sensitive; I remember dining on a restaurant patio and watching an officer hassle a group of Black boys on bicycles. They were children, between about eight and ten years old.

When I was a new attorney in 2005, my first job was at the city of Cleveland Heights law department. I worked in a department with four other attorneys. I was the youngest, by far, and the only Black attorney in the department. The department was never a comfortable space for me. My lone female colleague was a middle-aged woman who often told me how lucky I was to be Black because it helped me get accepted to my Ivy League alma mater. Between comments like these and the normal learning curve for a new lawyer, I was uneasy from the start.

Most of my coworkers claimed to be liberal, but the attitudes toward race that pervaded the office never sat well with me. The entire body of my career at Cleveland Heights centered upon police misconduct litigation involving young, Black males. Their stories haunt me to this day, as I remember the way their mothers looked at me sitting on the other side of the table. I felt like a token, and I was ashamed.

I remember learning of an instance of two middle school boys walking in a Cleveland Heights neighborhood; in fact, it was my neighborhood. The boys were walking from their church to a nearby movie theater. An officer in a police cruiser stopped them. The officer asked them for identification. They could not show him any (because most thirteen-year-olds don't carry identification), so he asked them where they lived. When one boy answered that he lived in a very affluent suburb, the officer assumed he was lying. The children ended up in the back of the car, crying, and were prevented from calling their parents.

The boys were eventually released without any further incident. The families, as one may imagine, were shaken and angry about their children's treatment. The father of the boy from the affluent town was a well-respected attorney with a prestigious position.

After the incident, the law director, an elderly, affluent, and often cantankerous white man, called me into his office. He asked me with all earnestness if I understood why the parents were so upset. In his view, the children were stopped by the officer, their answers to his questions were "evasive" (the word the officer used in his report), and they were eventually released without incident. He wondered why the parents were still upset and causing problems for the law department.

I blinked in silence for a moment, bewildered. I tried hard to formulate an answer to his question. I responded that the demeanor the officer characterized as evasive might have been out of fear. I don't remember what else I said, because I was too busy trembling and wishing the conversation would end.

That was only one of many similar interactions between the Cleveland Heights police and young Black people. One young man was stopped by an officer for driving at dusk without his lights fully illuminated. His mother was in the passenger seat. The stop was tense, and the officer told the young man's mother to shut up repeatedly.[28] When the young man told the officer not to tell his mother to shut up, he was arrested. The young man was driving his mother home from buying sheet music for their church choir, and he ended up in jail.

My employment at Cleveland Heights was not the only place that I learned about troubling incidents between police officers and innocent Black males. A teenager who attended my Cleveland Heights church sold raffle tickets to benefit his football team in his affluent neighborhood (coincidentally, he lived in a town adjacent to the boy in my first anecdote). His younger brother accompanied him to sell tickets door to door. A neighbor called the police to report the boys as suspicious characters. When officers arrived, they approached the children with guns drawn.[29]

I am sure there are many more similar stories about which I have no knowledge. I quit my job at Cleveland Heights less than two years after I started. After my short tenure, I decided that living in that city was not a safe place for me to raise Black children. As a result, my family relocated shortly after the birth of my first and only child. Considering the fate of Tamir Rice, I don't believe that much has changed in the decade since I moved away from northeast Ohio.

28. Knox v. Hetrick.
29. Nowak, "Forest Hill Church Conversations on Race."

JESUS AND MARY

Black motherhood comes with the curse of constant fear for the safety of our children. What if someone reports them as suspicious? What if the police think they have a gun? What if the officer insists that they look like threatening adults? However, in addition to the fear, we must also endure the knowledge that we would not likely see justice if our fear became realized. We must endure living in a system where if an officer shoots our unarmed child, we will be slandered, demeaned, and blamed. We can't be sure that anyone will seek justice for our children, and we may never be seen as mothering well enough.

Jesus experienced a brutal, shameful, and shocking form of death through the crucifixion. In first-century Palestine, death on the cross was the most dishonorable form of death one could experience.[30] Mary had to witness her son's slow and gruesome death. At the same time, she had to witness his derision by those who mocked him and put him to death. Women like Mamie Till and Samaria Rice share a common bond with Mary, bound together in a shared experience that no one should endure.

Like Mary, many Black mothers have experienced the violent death of a child. But instead of sympathy, they receive scorn. Instead of honor, they are reviled. Though these ordinary children are not messiahs, they are symbols of the cultural norms that devalue Black lives and Black loss; and I believe Christ's story can teach us something valuable on this subject.

The first Christians reacted to the unexpectedly shameful death that their Messiah endured. Jesus was a political pariah, and in the first century, death on a cross was the considered a disgraceful fate. However, the early church felt that it was through enduring this lowliness that Jesus was exalted. Through his shame he became Lord. In Paul's Letter to the Galatians, he emphasizes the fact that the ridicule and suffering experienced by Christ and the members of the early church were not shameful. Speaking of Christ's crucifixion, scholar David DiSilva says, "the society that held him in contempt was unaware of what was truly valuable and honorable in God's sight."[31] Paul's ideology embraces this concept as he boldly faces the cross, and sees it as representative of the truth and sacrifice in Christianity.

---

30. See Neyrey, "Despising the Shame of the Cross"; Hengel, "Crucifixion in the Ancient World"; and Goodacre, "Mark's Crucifixion Narrative."

31. DeSilva, *Hope of Glory*, 164–65.

Bearing this view of the cross in mind, the mothers of Black children killed by the powerful empire of whiteness may have more in common with Mary than they know. She may hold the key to turning pain and contempt into maternal grace.

Black women have always been able to identify with Christ's death on the cross, viewing his suffering as representative of their own. They cannot, however, easily relate to the reverence Mary has received as a grieving mother. The classical Mary is simply not a relevant figure for Black women. But that doesn't mean that she is useless. On the contrary, Mary offers a great deal for Black Christian mothers as a source of feminine spiritual influence. Like Mary, many Black women are known to treat the news of pregnancy as a reason to rejoice, even in the midst of imperfect family or financial situations. Like Mary, we sing a song of freedom to God. Like Mary, our faith runs deep, and we have believed in Jesus from the first moment we knew him. Like Mary, we ponder at times, worried about the violent, unjust world our children face. There is comfort we may find in Mary's story. What Black mothers require is a new way to look at Mary. What we need is a womanist Mariology.

10

WOMANIST THEOLOGY AND BIBLICAL INTERPRETATION

WOMANIST

1. From *womanish*. (Opp. of "girlish," i.e. frivolous, irresponsible, not serious.) A Black feminist or feminist of color. From the Black folk expression of mothers to female children, "you acting womanish," i.e., like a woman. Usually referring to outrageous, audacious, courageous or *willful* behavior. Wanting to know more and in greater depth than is considered "good" for one. Interested in grown up doings. Acting grown up. Being grown up. Interchangeable with another Black folk expression: "You trying to be grown." Responsible. In charge. *Serious.*

2. *Also:* A woman who loves other women, sexually and/or nonsexually. Appreciates and prefers women's culture, women's emotional flexibility (values tears as natural counterbalance of laughter), and women's strength. Sometimes loves individual men, sexually and/or nonsexually. Committed to survival and wholeness of entire people, male *and* female. Not a separatist, except periodically, for health. Traditionally a universalist, as in: "Mama, why are we brown, pink, and yellow, and our cousins are white, beige and black?" Ans.

"Well, you know the colored race is just like a flower garden, with every color flower represented." Traditionally capable, as in: "Mama, I'm walking to Canada and I'm taking you and a bunch of other slaves with me." Reply: "It wouldn't be the first time."

3. Loves music. Loves dance. Loves the moon. *Loves* the Spirit. Loves love and food and roundness. Loves struggle. *Loves* the Folk. Loves herself. *Regardless.*

4. Womanist is to feminist as purple is to lavender. —Alice Walker's *In Search of Our Mother's Gardens*.[1]

Alice Walker's definition of womanism is as deep, distinctive, and nebulous as the academic discipline itself. With scholars working throughout various fields of study, womanism is a way to engage in scholarship in virtually any area. The tie that binds all womanist scholarship is the starting point: the lived experiences of Black women. Also present is a common distrust of white feminism because of the racism that has existed in the movement as well as the lack of Black female access at feminism's conception. Similarly, there is a sense of exclusion from general Black liberation studies, because of the patriarchy historically at play in Black academic disciplines. My own point of view for womanism also includes an assumption of the existence of *misogynoir*, a form of misogyny that is uniquely and particularly experienced by Black women, based on a synthesis of social problems that *specifically* affect Black women. These include, but are not limited to, unique experiences of racialized sexual abuse, body shaming, workplace trauma, masculinization, broken family structures and standards of beauty.

The Black female experience is a starting point for doing womanist theology as well as biblical scholarship. The distinguished womanist ethicist Emilie Townes tells us that womanist theology is intentionally and unapologetically biased, and that all forms of theological discourse are open for reconsideration and critique.[2] Process theologian Monica Coleman focuses on womanist theology's proper placement being within postmodern thought and not modernist theology, which is limited in scope.[3]

Womanist biblical interpretation considers the historical and cultural contexts of biblical texts and evaluates them from the perspective of Black

1. Walker, *In Search of Our Mothers' Gardens*, xi–ii.
2. Townes, "Creating Ruminations from the Soul," introduction.
3. Coleman, *Making a Way*, 3.

womanhood. In *An Introduction to Womanist Biblical Interpretation*, Nyasha Junior teaches that womanist biblical scholarship is distinguished by the limited use of biblical texts, relying heavily upon the hermeneutic through which the Scripture is analyzed.[4] It is my observation that this womanist biblical analysis is almost always conducted using a hermeneutic of suspicion. This is based on the way that biblical texts have been historically leveraged against Black women to promote misogynoir.

Junior also highlights the fact that womanist biblical studies lack precise definition or standard methodology, that womanist biblical scholars are self-identified, and that their work has not had a significant impact on the production of scholarly contributions to the academy.[5] Junior points out the problem of paucity regarding the body of womanist biblical work, noting that only two monographs exist that are specifically identified as womanist biblical interpretation and that there is no scholarly journal dedicated to the topic.[6]

I will attempt to give an overview of key womanist theological and biblical study influencers. The following section carefully includes a sample of women who predate access to scholarship as well as scholars that work within an academic womanist sphere of influence; this list is by no means complete or exhaustive.

The concept of feminism is often divided into waves. Though womanist theological and biblical work is relatively young as an academic discipline, there are several pioneers that I consider to be the groundbreakers in Black female thought. These women pre-date the presence of Black women's access to the academy; I identify them as the first wave of womanist thinkers.

SLAVE NARRATIVES

During the period of Black enslavement, there is a lack of recorded Black experiences. Illiteracy and lack of opportunity prevented such work. However, the slave narratives that do exist were mostly given by women. Though these women did not intend to create theology, elements of womanist theology are present. Devotion to God, especially through Christ, is a common theme. The narratives create a theology motivated by Black female suffering and rooted in religious dedication and spiritual fervor.

4. Junior, *Introduction to Womanist Biblical Interpretation*, 59, 68–69, 100–102.

5. Ibid., 117.

6. Ibid., 114, 117.

In the narrative *Elizabeth, a Colored Minister of the Gospel, Born in Slavery*, a woman born around 1766 gives a detailed account of her life in bondage and her spiritual experience. Elizabeth's parents were religious Methodists who taught her from the Bible from childhood; she remembers feeling the Spirit at a young age even though she did not understand the meaning of the biblical lessons.[7] Elizabeth also tells of severe depression as an adolescent and adult, complete with suicidal ideations.[8] In battling her "melancholy," as she describes it, she tapped into her faith in God, believing it to be her only true support.

> ... as my mother said, I had none in the world to look to but God, I betook myself to prayer, and in every lonely place I found an altar. I mourned sore like a dove and chattered forth my sorrow, moaning in the corners of the field, and under the fences ... I saw with my spiritual eye, an awful gulf of misery. As I thought I was about to plunge into it, I heard a voice saying, "rise up and pray," which strengthened me. I fell on my knees and prayed the best I could the Lord's prayer. Knowing no more to say, I halted, but continued on my knees. My spirit was then taught to pray, "Lord have mercy on me—Christ save me" ... I was at this time not yet thirteen years old. The next day, when I had come to myself, I felt like a new creature in Christ, and all my desire was to see the Saviour.[9]

Though Elizabeth's call from the Spirit to preach the gospel to others pulled her strongly, she resisted the call. Eventually, she describes giving into the irresistible call of the Spirit:

> I felt at times that I must exercise in the ministry, but when I rose upon my feet I felt ashamed, and so I went under a cloud for some time, and endeavored to keep silence; but I could not quench the Spirit ... [T]he Spirit came upon me with life, and a victory was gained over the power of darkness, and we could rejoice together in his love ... Thus we see when the heart is not inspired, and the inward eye enlightened by the Spirit, we are incapable of discerning the mystery of God in these things.[10]

After a life of communion with the Spirit, as she approached death, Elizabeth reflected on the suffering of her life and her desire to leave her

---

7. Elizabeth, *Elizabeth, a Colored Minister*, 1.

8. Ibid., 3.

9. Ibid., 3–4.

10. Ibid., 7–8.

earthly struggles to enter "Jerusalem."[11] She deliberately and affirmatively declared her suffering's end and her sureness in her "eternal salvation":

> Two hours before her close, her mind being quite clear, she said, "My body is full of pain all over. I long for Jerusalem my home. I long to see my Saviour's face. My shackles are broken. Suffering has washed my robes and made them white in the blood of the Lamb: now let me be quiet for two hours." At the end of that time her breathing gently ceased; and without doubt her ransomed spirit entered through the pearly gates into that glorious city where none can say, I am sick; aged nearly 101 years.[12]

Elizabeth's beliefs defined her life, centered around two particular keystones: her suffering and the undeniable presence of the Spirit. This Spirit-driven theology allowed enslaved women to experience total freedom from an authority that surpassed all human authority, especially that of their masters. The Spirit in its unquenchable power proved itself the agent of a true Lord who could deliver them from their earthly suffering.

Another enslaved woman, named Octavia V. Rogers Albert, who lived from around 1853 to 1889, gave accounts of the stark contrast between the hell of her reality and the promise of heavenly salvation:

> But, I tell you, I believe there is only two places for us—heaven and torment. If we miss heaven we must be forever lost. . .Aunt Jane used to tell us, too, that the children of Israel was in Egypt in bondage, and that God delivered them out of Egypt; and she said he would deliver us.
>
> We all used to sing a hymn like this:
> "My God delivered Daniel, Daniel, Daniel;
> My God delivered Daniel,
> And why not deliver me too?
> He delivered Daniel from the lions' den,
> Jonah from the belly of the whale,
> The three Hebrew children from the fiery furnace,
> And why not deliver me too?"
>
> O, you ought to hear Richard sing that hymn! I never can forget Aunt Jane, for when old marster [sic] used to be so hard on me it seemed I'd have to give up sometimes and die. But then the Spirit

---

11. Ibid., 13, 16.
12. Ibid., 16.

of God would come to me and fill my heart with joy. It seemed the more trials I had the more I could pray.[13]

Like Elizabeth, Octavia too felt the powerful healing presence of the Spirit during her most difficult times. The combination of Black female suffering with a highly spiritualized experience of God shapes the theology of enslaved women. The theology these women, organically created, is akin to what is known as "Spirit Christology," in which the saving Spirit of God enters and deeply impacts individual and community lives. In *Sexism and God-Talk*, Rosemary Radford Ruether considers the focus on the prophetic Spirit in the early church.[14] The book of Acts provides an example of the importance of the prophetic Spirit for the apostolic church and their theology. It notably includes the detail that the Spirit will be poured out for both *women and men*, who will prophesy as a result:

> Even upon my slaves, both men and women, in those days I will pour out my Spirit; and they shall prophesy . . . Then everyone who calls on the name of the Lord shall be saved. (Acts 2:18, 21)

Ruether cites the patriarchalization of Christology during the first five centuries of the church as the main cause of the move from Spirit Christology to the orthodox Chalcedonian Christology that came to dominate the imperial, powerful church.[15] Because orthodoxy was established by a patriarchal empire, the marginal early church and their ecstatic expressions of Spirit encounters, as well as a focus on the forgiving and healing nature of Christ, was not present. The "Spirit-filled community" also lived in a highly eschatological mindset based on living in a truly fallen human condition that God would soon come to correct, and they would then "join a new heaven and earth that God will establish on a renewed earth."[16]

A connection exists between the earliest, largely illiterate and loosely organized apostolic churches, and slave communities in a similar situation, which makes perfect sense. The women of slave narratives confirm the existence of such a powerful theology for these womanist pioneers.

---

13. Albert, *House of Bondage*, 13.
14. Ruether, *Sexism and God-Talk*, 122–23.
15. Ibid., 122.
16 Ibid., 123.

Jarena Lee

Itinerant preacher Jarena Lee spent a great part of her life traveling throughout the United States and preaching the gospel. Born a free woman in 1783 in New Jersey, her socioeconomic status was nonetheless defined by her race, gender, poverty, and work as a servant.[17] Like her enslaved counterparts, Lee's faith experience was deeply rooted in a notion of the Spirit. In Lee's case, the Spirit called her to preach; a call that would compel her to travel and speak to audiences in a way that she otherwise would not have.[18] In this case, not only does the Spirit bring ecstasy and eschatological hope, it empowers actions that led to pushing the boundaries of societal oppression. On this liberation via Spirit, Albert Raboteau, professor of religion at Princeton University, writes:

> Jarena Lee's conversion is protracted—there's agonizing, and there's a refusal to obey the spirit, and then her eventual submission to the spirit—is a very intense and very visionary conversion experience. It's interesting because that's also the case with a number of other black women's conversion narratives in the 19th century—the strong emphasis on the spirit, and the spirit as empowering them to do something that is forbidden by the customs of the time, that is, to stand up and preach to mixed audiences ("mixed" here meaning men and women). And often this spirit also emboldens them to travel, to itinerate, to do something that is also not approved for women, especially because it means leaving their families—in Jarena's case leaving her child for extended periods of time to do the work of the spirit and to preach.[19]

Jarena Lee's homiletic work and focus on the Spirit theology developed by the Black women during the age of slavery places her among the first wave of womanist theologians.

Lee's spiritual conversion was spurred by her view of herself as a terribly lowly sinner, based sadly on a lie that she told her mistress, claiming that she had done a work task that in actuality she had not. This lie, which many would consider quite understandable and harmless, led Jarena to a place of guilt about her sinful nature.[20] Need for the redemption of Spirit

---

17. PBS, "Jarena Lee," lines 1–4.
18. Ibid., lines 11–19.
19. Raboteau, "On Jarena Lee."
20. Lee, "Religious Experience of Jarena Lee," lines 4–8.

based on guilt and self-doubt was also the impetus for the conversion of another well-known early womanist theologian.

Sojourner Truth

Perhaps the most well-known early womanist theologian is Sojourner Truth. Modern feminist scholar Elisabeth Schüssler Fiorenza cites Truth and her famous "Ain't I a Woman?" speech as a critical example of what Fiorenza labels as feminist theology, hermeneutics, and Christology.[21] Though Fiorenza places Truth within a feminist framework, I assert that Truth's theology is born out of the suffering experiences of Black female slavery (including violence and sexual abuse at the hands of white men and women), making it appropriately at home in a womanist context.[22]

The Narrative of Sojourner Truth details Truth's "trials" in life. Born as Isabella, the narrative centers on her experiences on the auction block, being physically abused and separated from her parents and children.[23] Like Jarena Lee, Isabella's conversion came after a dramatic spiritual experience. The living Jesus was revealed to Isabella in a vision, which took away the fear and dread of God that she previously held. She tells of her previous lies and her failure to recognize that God is present everywhere, even in hell, thus deserving her reverence and praise.[24]

Later in her narrative, after her name change, Sojourner returns to the idea that God (specifically through Jesus) is omnipotent and will walk with her through "the fire" that will consume the earth once the eschatological event takes place. "I am not going away; I am going to stay here and stand the fire . . . And Jesus will walk with me through the fire and keep me from harm . . . Do you tell me that God's children can't stand fire?"[25] Sojourner's relationship with the Spirit seemed to recognize that she was already living in a hell on earth, taking comfort in the presence of Jesus in the fire with her.

Sojourner Truth's preaching throughout her lifetime was highly prophetic. Along with her slavery era contemporaries, the Spirit permeated her

---

21. Schüssler Fiorenza, *Jesus Miriam's Child*, 62–63.

22. Ibid., 63.

23. Perry and Truth, *Narrative of Sojourner Truth*, 18.

24. Ibid., 48–49.

25. Ibid., 82.

theology. Truth's theology adheres to the prophetic Spirit-based beliefs of the apostolic church. Though Sojourner Truth aligned herself with white feminists throughout her career of preaching and activism, her theological outlook is consistent with that of the other women of the first wave.

Nancy Ambrose

A final member of the first wave is the grandmother of one of the most prolific formally educated theologians of the modern age: Howard Thurman. Thurman was raised by his grandmother, Nancy Ambrose, whose devout faith shaped his religious beliefs. Howard Thurman took his religious upbringing and became one of the first and most important Black theologians in the academy. In his work *Jesus and the Disinherited*, Thurman introduces us to his grandmother Nancy, who gives a succinct lesson in reading the Bible with a hermeneutic of suspicion:

> . . . during the days of slavery, . . . master's minister would occasionally hold services for the slaves. Always the white minister used as his text something from Paul. Slaves be obedient to your masters as unto Christ. Then he would go on to show that if we were good and happy slaves, God would bless us. I promised my maker that if I ever learned to read and if freedom ever came, I would not read that part of the bible.[26]

Ambrose was acutely aware of the fact that the "master's minister" was using Paul's epistles to uphold the oppressive structure that enslaved her. Though steadfast in faith, Nancy Ambrose read Scripture from a womanist perspective (or, one may argue, a Black liberation theological perspective). Her treatment of Scripture is an example of the textbook definition of womanist biblical interpretation given by Nyasha Junior in her primer. Ambrose deemphasizes the use of Scripture; in fact, she says she has no need to read that part of the Bible which was used to uphold her oppression. Ambrose also employs a hermeneutic of suspicion, obviously privy to the way in which the master's minister applied his own hermeneutic of oppression.

26. Thurman, *Jesus and the Disinherited*, 30–31; Hopkins and Thomas, *Walk Together Children*, 206.

ENTRY INTO SCHOLARSHIP: THE SECOND WAVE

After the end of slavery and Jim Crow, Black women eventually gained greater access to formal education and academia. Here we find the innovators of the scholarly discipline of womanist theology and biblical study that we have today. A far cry from the dictated slave narratives of illiterate women, you will find these women on social media and in collegiate classrooms. The scholars discussed in this section are by no means an exhaustive list of womanist theologians, ethicists, and biblical scholars. However, this group represents a cross section of work that heavily influences contemporary womanist scholarship.

Jacquelyn Grant

Jacquelyn Grant is considered a founding member of the school of womanist theology. Her seminal work *White Women's Christ and Black Women's Jesus: Feminist Christology and Womanist Response* offers a compelling case for a womanist theology that differs from both the feminist and male-centered Black liberation views of Christ. Grant's theology employs the importance of the intersectionality of the Black woman's experience, or as she names it, "tri-dimensional" experience of racism, sexism, and classism.[27] Grant teaches that Black women have traditionally identified with Jesus as a "divine co-sufferer," one who experienced great persecution and undeserved suffering as they have.[28] Because of his unique ability to empathize with oppression, Black women have consequently chosen Jesus as the face of the Trinity with whom they constantly choose to commune.

Grant connects her Christology of "the least" to that of the first-wave thinkers Jarena Lee and Sojourner Truth, both of whom closely identified with Jesus as the source of their liberation and salvation. Truth, who was not able to read the Bible, stated that the source of all of her preaching was "When I found Jesus!"[29] Likewise, Jarena Lee used Jesus' salvific act as the basis for defending a woman's right to preach, because Jesus died for "woman as well as for the man."[30] Grant's presentation of Black women's

27. Grant, *White Women's Christ and Black Women's Jesus*, 169.
28. Ibid., 171–72.
29. Ibid., 173.
30. Ibid., 177; Lee, "Religious Experience of Jarena Lee," 15–16.

Jesus demonstrates a view of Jesus that embodies one of the main experiences that defines womanist theology, namely, suffering.

Emilie Townes

Ethicist and theologian Emilie Townes writes on the idea of Black women's suffering and loss as the descriptive locus of Black womanhood. Townes argues that a womanist ethic rejects the notion of this suffering as God's will. She believes that suffering is an abomination and that a womanist ethic focuses on eradicating suffering.[31] In contrast to Grant's focus on suffering, Townes considers the Black church's historical love for the Hebrew scriptures that detail suffering, enslavement, and oppression of the Jewish people.[32] Townes believes this elevation of suffering makes it a virtuous act.[33] Townes instead challenges us to transform suffering into pain, viewing pain as a tool that may be used for empowerment and healing. For Townes, Jesus' triumph over death through the resurrection delivers us from the suffering of the cross into the triumph of the living Christ.

Delores Williams

Delores Williams wrote her classic text *Sisters in the Wilderness: The Challenge of Womanist God-Talk* over twentuy years ago, placing her in the small number of second-wave womanist theologians. Her book focuses on the experience of the biblical figure Hagar, the African slave woman who was forced to have a child with Abraham because his wife, Sarah, was infertile. After giving birth to her son, Ishmael, Sarah's jealousy and mistreatment forces Hagar to run away with her baby into the wilderness. Hagar's enslavement, abuse, and sexual-reproductive exploitation closely parallel the experience of the Black American woman. Williams also employs the concept today known as intersectionality, examining the racial, class, and gender issues that affected both Hagar and Black women from enslavement until the present.[34]

31. Townes, *Troubling in My Soul*, 78–85.

32. Ibid., 84.

33. The concept of suffering as a virtue is apparent in the tradition of Mariology, akin to the Muslim appreciation for the suffering of Maryam and Fatima discussed in chapter 6.

34. Williams, *Sisters in the Wilderness*.

Renita Weems

Renita Weems is a Hebrew Bible scholar who has been producing womanist biblical interpretation for decades. The first Black woman to earn a PhD in Old Testament studies, Weems describes her work as a combination of feminist biblical criticism and Black oral tradition.[35] Her 1988 work *Just a Sister Away* was the first book described as a womanist biblical interpretation, and is considered a groundbreaking work in the field.[36] Weems has produced a diverse body of work both within and outside of biblical scholarship, and her biblical work focuses on texts that prove particularly problematic for Black women.[37]

Clarice Martin

Clarice Martin is a New Testament scholar who has been active since the 1980s. Martin was the first Black woman to earn a PhD in New Testament studies, making her another pioneer in womanist biblical interpretation. Martin's work takes on issues in the New Testament such as the problematic concept of illustrating the faithful as slaves (*doulos*), which is used throughout the New Testament, as well as the household codes that appear in Paul's epistles.[38]

THE NEW SCHOOL: A THIRD WAVE CLOSE BEHIND

Monica Coleman

Monica Coleman is a thought leader in the third wave of womanist theologians. Her work is distinctive in that she works from a postmodern, process theology framework instead of the systematic theology used by most modern womanist theologians. Coleman's book *Making a Way Out of No Way: A Womanist Theology* seeks to create a womanist theology located squarely within postmodernity, a perspective that Coleman views as more socially

---

35. Junior, *Introduction to Womanist Biblical Interpretation*, 95.
36. Ibid., 97.
37. Ibid., 98–99.
38. Ibid., 103.

conscious than modern thinking.[39] This consciousness causes postmodern thinkers to consider the particularity of one's experience as vital. Process theology is a postmodern discipline that considers the ways the past, the present situation, and the possibilities for future action impact any situation. Process theology focuses on what is possible for one to achieve within one's context; God's role is to offer us the possibilities, not to manipulate or control events externally.[40] Coleman argues that what we do has an effect on God and the way God relates to us.[41]

Kelly Brown Douglas

Kelly Brown Douglas offers work that closely relates to contemporary incidences of Black bodies as victims of racialized violence. Her work on bodies and theology also extends to the consideration of Black bodies and their treatment within the institutional Black church. Her recent work *Stand Your Ground: Black Bodies and the Justice of God* examines the supremacist structures within American society and the way that Black bodies are viewed as inherently guilty or worthless. Her most influential work, however, is *The Black Christ*, in which Douglas delves into the complex historical relationship between Christ and Black people. The "Black Christ" acts as a liberator; like Grant, Douglas presents a Christ who is a divine co-sufferer.

Nyasha Junior

Nyasha Junior is a Hebrew Bible scholar who in 2015 gave us a comprehensive overview of womanist biblical interpretation in *An Introduction to Womanist Biblical Interpretation*. Junior describes the hermeneutic used in womanist readings of the Bible and also does a good job describing the history of womanism in all areas of the religious studies academy. Junior's book points out the fact that womanist Biblical work borrows heavily from womanist theology and ethics because of the small number of Black women working as biblical scholars. Junior also shows us that those I named in the second wave of womanist scholarship are still producing work, demonstrating the infancy of these areas of study.

39. Coleman, *Making a Way*, 7.
40. Ibid, 8–9, 45–46.
41. Ibid., 52.

Wil Gafney

Wil Gafney is a Hebrew Bible scholar whose 2006 work *A Black Feminist Approach to Biblical Studies* employs her own approach to womanism. Gafney's work focuses on multidimensionality: experience, social location of the reader, and the importance of making scholarship available to the "wider nonspecialist worshipping community."[42] Gafney's work creates what she refers to as a "womanist midrash," which combines the Black female worldview and imagination with the ancient rabbinic tradition of midrash.[43]

Shanell Smith

Shanell Smith is among the first New Testament scholars in the third wave of womanist scholarship. On faculty at Hartford Seminary, Smith's work has focused on the "Woman Babylon" (also commonly known as the Whore of Babylon) in the book of Revelation. In *The Woman Babylon and the Marks of Empire: Reading Revelation with a Postcolonial Womanist Hermeneutics of Ambiveilance*, Smith introduces the innovative concept of reading biblical texts "ambi*veil*antly." She defines this term as a combination of the concept of the veil presented by W. E. B. Du Bois[44] and the concept of colonial ambivalence expressed by postcolonial specialist Homi Bhabha. Combining the two concepts, Smith coins ambi*veil*ance. As a result, a hermeneutic emerges that accounts for the individualized, nuanced, and culturally contextual way in which readers interpret the text.

CONCLUSION

From the wisdom of illiterate, enslaved women to the postmodern scholar, the body of womanist theological and biblical studies work shares some common threads that bind the discipline as well as the worldview together. Each woman's work described in this chapter includes an emphasis on

42. " Junior, *Introduction to Womanist Biblical Interpretation*, 109; Gafney, *Black Feminist Approach*, 392.

43. Gafney, *Black Feminist Approach*, 52.

44. Du Bois describes the veil as a distorting screen through which white Americans view Blacks, and also a screen through which Blacks view the world and themselves, based on their social location as an oppressed minority. See Du Bois, *Souls of Black Folk*, 195. Bhabha discusses the nuanced colonial ambivalence that oscillates between mimicry and menace in his essay "Of Mimicry and Man."

the Black woman's experience, especially through physical, mental, and emotional pain and suffering. These women always apply a hermeneutic of suspicion, astutely aware that the previous mainstream constructs often cut against the interests of Black women. The work also addresses Black women's bodies as centuries-old sites of abuse, sexual violation, and vulnerable pregnancies. The issue of Black women's bodies is one that has a significant effect as we travel on toward a womanist Mariology.

11

BLACK BODIES AND
THE VIRGINITY PROBLEM

Mary's virginity poses a challenge for any woman who seeks to emulate her. The miraculous nature of the virgin conception and birth cannot be replicated by ordinary women. The idea of perpetual virginity in a marriage is also impractical. Though these are impossibilities for any women, Black women must overcome the particularized problem of inhabiting bodies that have historically been oppressed.

For Black women, the body is loaded with complicated baggage. From the time Black women were captured by slave traders, body autonomy disappeared. When placed on display on the auction block, their naked bodies were available to be poked, prodded, and examined before they were finally sold as chattel. During enslavement, Black women lost virtually all self-determination and body control. Their bodies were abused, commodified, and policed reproductively, sexually, and physically. With treatment as high-yielding breeders and wet nurses, back-breaking field work, physical beatings, and sexual exploitation, enslaved women's bodies were disrespected and disregarded by an entire society.

An example of the magnitude of the degradation and abuse of Black women's bodies exists in the tragic story of late eighteenth-century woman Saartjie Baartman.[1] Known as the "Hottentot Venus," Baartman's body experienced unspeakable exploitation for the duration of her short life. She was a member of the *Khoikhoi* people of southwestern Africa, who were

1. Saartjie Baartman is also known as Sarah Baartman.

offensively dubbed "Hottentots" by European occupiers. With peaked pru-
rient interest in Baartman's posterior and allegedly enlarged labia, a free
Black man and a British military surgeon named William Dunlop took
Baartman to Europe as a freak show attraction. In the shows, she was forced
to display her immodestly dressed body, sing, and dance. At times she was
taken to private homes for special showings where guests were allowed to
touch her body.[2]

After moving to France, Baartman became a source of interest for the
French medical community. A physician named Georges Cuvier took a
particular interest in Baartman. Inspired by Cuvier, several French doctors
examined her body, seeking to observe the supposed differences between
African and European bodies.[3]

Some sources claim Baartman may have turned to sex work upon fac-
ing financial troubles late in her life. Eventually developing substance abuse
problems with alcohol or opiates, Baartman died in 1815. Her cause of
death is unconfirmed, but she suffered from an illness that may have been
syphilis or small pox. Baartman's bodily exploitation at the hands of white
men did not end with her death. Cuvier made a plaster cast of her body,
removed her skeleton, and pickled her brain and genitals, placing them in
glass jars to be displayed at the Musee de l'Homme in Paris. Her body parts
remained on display until 1974; in 1994 President Nelson Mandela called
for Baartman's remains to be returned to her homeland, where they would
be respectfully laid to rest.[4]

After the end of slavery in the diaspora, the treatment of Black women's
bodies as public spaces has persisted. Black women still experience racialized objectification and abuse, which permeates many areas of society. In
this section, we will consider several recent incidences that exhibit the ways
in which Black female bodies and their images are subject to a particularized abuse.

NICKI MINAJ

Popular hip-hop artist Nicki Minaj is known for her self-confident irrever-
ence and also for the size and shape of her posterior. Minaj's body is her
pop culture trademark; in the music video for her hit song "Anaconda," she

2. Parkinson, "Significance of Sarah Baartman."
3. Ibid.
4. Ibid.

appears dancing on all fours with her buttocks exposed. While Minaj's body depiction is within her control, society has treated images of her body in ways that are reminiscent of Saartjie Baartman.

A 2015 skit on the Ellen DeGeneres show featured actors portraying a child Nicki Minaj and her parents; all had exaggerated, padded backsides. The girl who portrayed young Nicki looked nothing like her. Darker skinned and with kinkier hair, the grades school–aged girl was featured in tight pink pants with an extremely large, curved padded rear end. Critics pointed out the willingness of those who produced the skit to sexualize and objectify the body of a young Black girl.

A wax statue likeness of Nicki Minaj was installed at the famous Madame Tussaud's in 2015. The statue is posed with Minaj on all fours presenting her backside as she does in the "Anaconda" video. After the introduction of the statute, guests at the attraction quickly began taking inappropriate photos with the figure, simulating various sexual acts with the figure.[5] These photos elicit thoughts of Saartjie Baartman placed on display for sexual thrills and general public amusement.

A SUBTLETY: THE MARVELOUS SUGAR BABY

During the 2014 Brooklyn summer, MacArthur "genius" grant-winning artist Kara Walker installed a massive sculpture made of sugar in an old Domino sugar factory. Shaped as a Sphinx with large hands out front, the figure depicts a woman with pronounced facial features such as a wide nose and big lips. It also has large breasts protruding out front, and a back view including the figure's buttocks and labia. The woman's head resembles a "Mammy" or "Aunt Jemima" complete with kerchief and earrings. According to the curatorial statement provided by Creative Time, this massive "Sphinx-turned-Mammy" made of pure white sugar evokes imagery of the Black woman who has been treated as both caregivers for white families and as an oversexualized sex object. The sugar also raises the notion of the sugar trade and those who historically participated in its production.[6]

Unsurprisingly, the "Sugar Baby's" anatomy was objectified by some visitors, who took crude selfies near her breasts or vulva. Many of these visitors were white, adding a layer of racial tension to such actions. After the short exhibit had closed, Walker revealed that she had footage from a

5. Machado, "Nicki Minaj's Wax Figure."
6. Thompson, "Curatorial Statement."

camera crew whom she had previously instructed to record patrons of the exhibit. The footage was compiled into a documentary that Walker named *An Audience*. Walker explained her film to *Los Angeles Times* writer Carolina A. Miranda:

> I put a giant 10-foot vagina in the world and people respond to giant 10-foot vaginas in the way that they do. It's not unexpected. Maybe I'm sick. Sometimes I get a sort of kick out of the hyper essay writing, that there's gotta be this way to sort of control human behavior. [But] human behavior is so mucky and violent and messed-up and inappropriate. And I think my work draws on that. It comes from there. It comes from responding to situations like that, and it pulls it out of an audience. I've got a lot of video footage of that [behavior]. I was spying.[7]

Another modern Saartjie Baartman phenomenon, *A Subtlety or the Marvelous Sugar Baby* showed us the ways that even a twenty-first-century crowd in Williamsburg, Brooklyn, could be mesmerized and amused by the Black female body, and acted in a manner that mimicked exploitation.

TEXAS POOL PARTY

A 2015 incident in a suburban subdivision in McKinney, Texas, made national headlines when a white male police officer was filmed throwing a Black bikini-clad teen to the ground, pressing his knee into her back and drawing his gun, after neighbors called in complaints of a loud group of teens who were suspected to be using the private neighborhood pool without authorization. The crowd of children dispersed when police arrived, but the girl in question told local news, "He told me to keep walking, and I kept walking. And then, I'm guessing he thought we were saying rude stuff to him." She described how the officer twisted her around her back, how he pulled her hair and hurt her back. She added, "Him getting fired is not enough."[8]

The image of an armed adult white male physically attacking a young Black girl was unsettling; however, the fact that her swimsuit exposed much of her body adds to the egregious dynamic displayed between this officer and child. A girl being manhandled while dressed in a vulnerable way evokes images of the physical and sexual abuse that many young Black girls

7. Miranda, "Q&A with Kara Walker."
8. Chappell, "Texas Pool Party Update."

and women have experienced at the hands of white men with authority over them.[9]

DANIEL HOLTZCLAW AND THE #SAYHERNAME MOVEMENT

Oklahoma police officer Daniel Holtzclaw was convicted on eighteen of the thirty-six charges brought against him for the rape and sexual assault of thirteen different Black women.[10] The victims of his heinous crimes were often drug users or sex workers, usually in their forties and fifties. According to reports regarding Holtzclaw's defense, the women were the ones put on trial. Defense attorney Adams challenged the women, several of whom appeared in orange prison jumpsuits, questioning their credibility. Adams questioned every inconsistency in testimony, focused on their drug use, and especially wondered why they would wait to come forward until they were contacted by investigators. One woman responded while crying, "What's the good of telling the police? What kind of police do you call on the police?"[11] Adams responded with, "You could have called anybody at 911 and said, 'Not only was I raped by an Oklahoma City police officer, but I have DNA evidence all over the place in my room.'"[12] The youngest accuser, who was eighteen at the trial and a minor at the time of her assault, said, "I'm really getting upset by the way you're coming after me."[13] Though Holtzclaw was found guilty of some, but not all, of his charges, Black women were revictimized by a white man while they testified against their assailant.

While the Black Lives Matter movement has been a hot topic in public dialogue, the much less-publicized Say Her Name movement has also emerged, gaining and keeping most of its traction on social media. When mainstream media uses the term "Black Lives Matter"—a term created by Black women—it is usually to highlight racialized violence against Black men. Say Her Name points out that Black women are even yet further

---

9. I do not wish to imply that there was anything wrong with the girl's swim attire or that I wish to police her dress. I do, however, believe that her relative lack of coverage contributes to the violation of her body by the officer's actions.

10. Larimer, "Holtzclaw Sentenced to 263 Years."

11. Merchant and Talley, "Defense Questions Credibility."

12. Ibid.

13. Ibid.

marginalized by American society. The history of racialized sexual abuse toward Black women looms over victims like Holtzclaw's, whose abuses are often invisible. Those who are not only Black but women and socially outcast, too, carry intersecting and inseparable identities of societal disadvantage. Though the Black Lives Matter movement has made a concerted effort to include all Black voices, there is still a need for an intersectional approach to the particular problem of Black women and police violence.

STREET HARASSMENT AND SPIRIT MURDER

Street harassment is yet another way in which Black women and their bodies are violated on a daily basis. In *The Harm That Has No Name: Street Harassment, Embodiment, and African American Women*, legal scholar Deirdre Davis takes on the enduring topic of street harassment. While women of all races experience street harassment, Davis argues that the inclusion of Black women in the discourse on the topic is both necessary and valuable to the conversation. Davis's article considers of some of the issues discussed in earlier chapters such as the context of the historical invasion of Black women's bodies by white men applying the Jezebel stereotype, and the treatment of Black female bodies as commodified breeding machines.[14]

Davis astutely considers the "cult of true womanhood," which upholds white standards of female value while diminishing the value of Black women. Davis applies a new definition of the harm caused by street harassment that also applies broadly to situations involving the mistreatment of Black women's bodies: "spirit murder."[15]

Deirdre Davis is a highly educated and accomplished woman. However, she shares her daily experiences as a Black woman as examples of "spirit murder." The systemic misogynoir that she encounters—being followed by a suspicious salesperson in a store, being told she "doesn't seem Black," and receiving hostility toward her interracial relationship—cause Davis to "die a little death each time" she has these experiences.[16]

Davis borrows the term "spirit murder" from legal scholar Patricia Williams, whose work *Spirit-Murdering the Messenger: The Discourse of Fingerpointing as the Law's Response to Racism* considers daily, systemic racism as a form of murder as invidious as physical murder. Like Davis,

14. Davis, "Street Harassment, Embodiment," 136, 166.
15. Ibid., 177.
16. Ibid.

Williams describes the humiliation of the racist treatment she receives, detailing one particular instance when she was denied entrance to a New York City shop by a white teenage clerk.[17] Williams then examines the law and society's tendency to "spirit murder" messengers who experience and report incidences of racial trauma by legitimizing racism through attempts to justify the negative stereotypes placed on Blacks. In Williams's store example, she cites the way that people justify racial profiling of customers as a necessary evil to prevent crime while ignoring the racism in implying that Blacks are more likely to engage in criminal behavior. This scenario also fails to label the "spirit murder" effect of racism as blameworthy, criminally or otherwise.

THE VIRGINITY PROBLEM

In stark contrast, the prevailing cultic images of Mary as a white virgin queen were born entirely from within a different societal framework. The "cult of true womanhood" was an entirely white phenomenon. The idea of women as the "fairer sex" or the "weaker sex" applied only to white women. The cult of true womanhood placed the patriarchal concept of an idealized woman on a pedestal to be glorified and cherished while simultaneously being socially controlled. The Marian images created by the Marian cult are wholly a product of the cult of true womanhood. With that, Mary is entrenched in whiteness. Mary's perpetual, intact virginity stands in stark opposition to demeaned Black bodies like Saartjie Baartman's.

In the twenty-first century, the cult of true womanhood persists in Christianity, appearing now as "purity culture." Largely a byproduct of doctrinally conservative evangelical theology, purity culture places an extremely high value on female "virtue."[18] Purity includes complete abstention from sexual contact, but can also go as far as prohibiting kissing, hugging, or hand holding before marriage. With fathers seen as the guardians of the chastity of their daughters, girls may receive a purity ring from their father, or sign a contract pledging to remain "pure" until their sexuality is gifted to their husband. Using language that often invokes images of purity as "white as snow," the purity culture is not applicable, accessible, or relatable for girls and women of color.

17. Williams, "Spirit-Murdering the Messenger," 128.

18. While I acknowledge that purity culture also has real effects on males in the church, the emphasis on purity is mainly directed at girls and women.

Where then, does Mary's virginity fit into a womanist Mariology? How can Black women, whose bodies bear the burden of centuries of disrespect, reconcile a prototype for Christian womanhood that is unrealistically pure?

A womanist Mariology must eliminate the fixation on Mary's virginity as a central tenet. Chalcedonian Christology includes the fact of Mary's virginity as a sign that Jesus was divinely conceived. Born of a virgin, Jesus was fully human and fully divine from the time he was conceived. The addition of the concept of Mary's perpetual virginity is not stated in the gospels, and the texts refer to Jesus' brothers. Her perpetual virginity was assigned extra-biblically, and out of an early European church rife with the cult of true womanhood and patriarchal understandings of feminine purity.

Mary's virginity is christologically necessary. However, a womanist Mary is not eternally virgin. Instead, she is a prophetic, miraculous woman. She is a woman of a low caste and an oppressed ethnicity. She is a girl who today would be labeled "at risk." She is a mother of loss who watched her son die at the hands of the state. She is a young mother whose steadfast faith stayed with her as she pondered the fate of her son. This Mary is no bejeweled lifelong virgin. She is one who would be *excluded* from the cult of true womanhood, not its leader.

What then do we make of the "visitation," when the Spirit of God came upon Mary, impregnating her? In a womanist paradigm, Mary's lack of sexual-reproductive agency is troubling. Like the young slave girls and nursemaids whose children were the products of rape by white men, Mary found herself pregnant without the full power of choice. Was the action of the Spirit just another patriarchal act of force without consent?

As discussed in a previous chapter, Elisabeth Schüssler Fiorenza considers the problematic nature of the visitation when constructing a feminist Mariology. What Mary experienced was indeed a form of "womb invasion," but the result was the Messiah.

Traditional Mariology solves the consent problem through placing emphasis on Mary's fiat, the moment when she accepted her role faithfully. However, for women who have experienced sexual violence and lack of sexual agency, the idea of faithfully accepting a womb invasion is still undesirable. Because of this, extra care must be taken to avoid the implication of permissible victim blaming. For ordinary women, the womb invasions they have experienced were non-consensual, violent, and coercive. A womanist Mariology must not romanticize or venerate victimization.

However, when Mary's fiat is considered a moment of saying yes *to her son*, the meaning changes. Mary happily accepted Jesus into her womb even though it was unexpected, unchosen, and socially unacceptable. Still, she rejoiced at her fortune and prepared to receive the gift of her son. When Mary traveled to the hill country to spend time with her kinswoman Elizabeth, she shared her joy through the recitation of her Magnificat. She shared the bonds of pregnancy with Elizabeth who had desired a child her whole life. Mary's unwed, unplanned pregnancy and Elizabeth's fertility miracle baby: both pregnancies were received with an immediate commitment to motherhood despite imperfect social circumstances. These women were honored to carry and bear sons in a fully human way, far outside of the cult of true womanhood.

The Black mothers whose children were fathered by their abusers accepted the role of mother nonetheless. Their personal sacrifices and pleading prayers for their children's well-being took center stage. Though their pregnancies may have been unwanted, inconvenient, or dangerous, they accepted motherhood. Today, the Black family is arguably matriarchal; Black mothers are still the core of their families. As they learned to make something out of nothing by cooking the undesirable cuts of meat, they also learned to mother well in the face of immense oppression.

A womanist Mariology must honor and name Mary's lack of agency. It must emphasize her resilience and devotion to motherhood instead of clinging to a notion of lifelong purity. It must also honor the ways Mary made something from nothing: a declaration of blessedness in the face of unplanned pregnancy, a nursery out of a manger, and eventually the faith to tell her son to make wine out of water. A womanist Mary is not perpetually virginal, but she is a mother who is as real as they come.

12

MAGNIFICAT—A FREEDOM SONG

My soul magnifies the Lord,
and my spirit rejoices in God my Savior,

for he has looked with favor on the lowliness of his servant.

Surely, from now on all generations will call me blessed;
for the Mighty One has done great things for me,
and holy is his name.

His mercy is for those who fear him
from generation to generation.

He has shown strength with his arm;
he has scattered the proud in the thoughts of their hearts.

He has brought down the powerful from their thrones,
and lifted up the lowly;

he has filled the hungry with good things,
and sent the rich away empty.

He has helped his servant Israel,
in remembrance of his mercy,

according to the promise he made to our ancestors,
to Abraham and to his descendants forever. (Luke 1:46–55)

Liberation theology is a discipline that examines systems of social, economic, and political oppression in relation to the gospel. A movement primarily founded and championed by Latin Americans, liberation theology has historically been Catholic in scope. Because of this,

Mariology has a significant place in liberation thought. An emphasis on Mary's Magnificat acts as a useful starting point for liberation theology.

This chapter considers Mary's Magnificat and its theological implications. After considering a brief summary of liberation thought, I will draw a parallel between a liberationist interpretation of the Magnificat and a womanist approach that treats the Magnificat as a freedom song for Black women. When viewed through a womanist lens, the Magnificat serves as the scriptural crux of a womanist Mariology.

GOD'S PREFERENTIAL TREATMENT OF THE POOR

Peruvian priest and theologian Gustavo Gutierréz is considered the father of liberation theology; his work *A Theology of Liberation* is the primer text. Gutierréz examines the theology of liberation, how it has historically been applied by the church, and the ways the church can change its behavior in the future to support a theology of liberation.

Gutierréz speaks of poverty as a "scandalous condition" as presented in the Bible, calling the condition "inimical to human dignity and therefore contrary to the will of God."[1] In an interview with *America* magazine, Gutierréz speaks of Mary's Magnificat as illustrative of this liberation philosophy: "[W]e can see from the Magnificat that, when Mary rejoices in God, she is also celebrating the liberating action of God in history. Mary rejoices in a God who is faithful to the poor. Our service of others must be wrapped in this joy. Only work embraced with joy truly transforms."[2]

Leonard Boff views Mary as a mother sharing the pain of the injustice that Jesus experienced in pursuit of not only redemption but liberation. Mary believes the rich and powerful will be "toppled from their places" and in the process will rediscover their humanity.[3] Bertrand de Margie quotes Victor Codina's liberationist view of Mary: "Mary personifies the preferential option of God for the Poor, for the weak, and for those who suffer . . . [A]bove all . . . Mary personifies the preference of God toward those who

---

1. Gutiérrez, *Theology of Liberation*, 165.
2. Hartnett, "Remembering the Poor."
3. Margerie, "Mary in Liberation Theologies," 55. See also Boff, *Way of the Cross*, 29–32.

suffer from the injustice of the powerful; she personifies the triumph of God in human weakness and his preference for the humanly insignificant."[4]

SONG OF HOPE

Both church and academy have made a connection between the Magnificat and the idea of hope. Pope Francis has stated that the Magnificat is a "song of hope" that is of particular value in areas "where the Body of Christ is suffering the Passion." For Pope Francis, there is no Christian faith without hope.[5]

In her doctoral dissertation given at the International Marian Research Institute, Mary Catherine Nolan distinguishes the Magnificat as a "post-resurrection hymn." She calls the moment of the visitation the intersection of the Old and New Covenants.[6] For Nolan, Mary's song offers the full scope of the hope inspired by the impending resurrection, and the eschatological hope given in Jesus Christ. The Magnificat acts as a "song of reversal," demonstrating the reversal of the order of the world caused by the incarnation. The last has become first as Mary has brought forth a liberator for the lowly.[7]

Matthew F. Morry echoes the idea that in the Magnificat, Mary offers a crucial reversal for the world. For Morry, the "poor of Yahweh" or the "remnant" are those who will receive God's preferential option for the poor. In her song, Mary offers the Poor of Yahweh a message of hope: that God, through fulfilling his promise of a savior, has offered a reason for "confident hope" that the needs of the poor will be met by the coming of God's kingdom.[8] Quoting Lucan scholar Joseph Fitzmyer, Morry shares this: "The 'poor' represent generically the neglected mass of humanity . . . The rich and poor in the Lucan writings symbolize, in effect the rejection and acceptance of Jesus the prophet announcing a new message of God's salvation and peace."[9]

This consideration of the expansion of the biblical meaning of "poor" is important in the application of liberation theories to a Womanist

4. Margerie, "Mary in Liberation Theologies."

5. "Mary Is with Us in Our Struggles."

6. Nolan, "Magnificat," 50.

7. Ibid., 54.

8 Morry, "Magnificat: Reflections," 66–67.

9. Ibid., 72. Fitzmyer, *Luke 1–9*, 250–51.

theology. Throughout history, Black women have been disproportionately economically poor. However, their systemic rejection and neglect reach beyond the scope of mere economics. This important idea prepares us for the consideration of Mary's Magnificat as a freedom song.

MAGNIFICAT: A FREEDOM SONG

All generations would call her blessed, but how about her own generation? They probably called her something else . . .[10]

Liberation scholar Virgilio Elizondo's thoughtful approach to Mary's story easily lends itself to a womanist Mariology. Elizondo opens his article "Mary in the Struggles of the Poor" considering the tarnished reputation that Mary no doubt developed after the visitation. He argues that God became incarnate by choosing to be born as a "despised and rejected" Galilean Jew, making Jesus the marginalized among the marginalized.[11] Just as Mary's reputation was likely damaged by her unwed pregnancy, Jesus was also on the receiving end of many abusive names.[12] With the label of "bastard" looming over him along with his subversive activities, Jesus had much in common with the young Black males who are stereotyped as "thugs" today. Like the mothers of Black males such as Trayvon Martin and Michael Brown, Mary likely received little sympathy for the death of her son. Like these women, perhaps Mary was even blamed for raising such a son.

Elizondo also takes on Mary's virginity in his analysis of Mary. Since Mary was a young, poor, unwed mother, the shame she would have experienced is akin to the shame many poor women bear when becoming mothers. This sense of being unworthy to be a mother or sexually "stained" or "ruined" is a major factor in a womanist Mariology. As examined in chapter 11, Mary's virginity poses a problem for Black women because of the way their sexual agency has been abused and violated by society. Elizondo offers a redemptive, restorative, and poignant solution to this problem: "God protects the powerless and defenseless to such a degree that what the world might prostitute, God can virginize . . . virginity has a dynamic and life-giving signification as the resurrection for it truly marks the experience of new life—the calling forth from the tombs of inferiority, illegitimacy, public

10. Elizondo, "Mary in the Struggles of the Poor," 4.
11. Ibid.
12. Ibid., 4–5.

sinfulness, unworthiness, moral disgrace."[13] For Elizondo, the "violated lives" of sexually abused marginalized women experience "virginal purity and joy" through Mary's blessedness.

Elizondo's liberation theology bridges the gap between the original liberation thought developed by Gutierréz and a womanist liberation theology. While liberation theology originally focused on the economically poor, the complexity of Black female identity moves beyond poverty to an entire identity of social rejection. The poverty within our social order that Black women experience is the basis for a womanist Mariology. This social poverty, as well as the relationships of Black women to those who are killed by state violence, places Black women in a particularized position that requires their liberation.

Mary's Magnificat serves as an anthem for Black women, declaring personal blessedness and worth along with intimate knowledge of God's preference for the oppressed. In the tradition of the spirituals sung by Harriet Tubman as she liberated the enslaved and the freedom songs of the 1960s that were the backdrop to the civil rights movement, the Magnificat is a freedom song. For Black women, Mary's words represent the sorely needed liberation that God delivers through Mary's motherhood of Jesus.

Few symbols of the New Testament's concern for "the least" are as powerful as the one shaped by Mary. It is fitting that she raised her voice from the margins and proclaimed to the world this powerful freedom song. Mary's freedom song is a vital part of the womanist Mariology created in this book. Armed with this song, we are finally ready to give birth to a womanist Mariology.

13. Ibid., 5.

13

BLACK MADONNA
A Manifesto of a Womanist Mariology

I am Black and beautiful,
O daughters of Jerusalem,
like the tents of Kedar,
like the curtains of Solomon.
Do not gaze at me because I am dark,
because the sun has gazed on me.
My mother's sons were angry with me;
they made me keeper of the vineyards,
but my own vineyard I have not kept! (Song 1:5–6)

We are now ready to give birth to a womanist Mariology. In doing so, M. Shawn Copland's formula for constructing a womanist theology of suffering acts as a useful starting place. For Copland, womanist theology that focuses on Black women's suffering consists of four elements: remembering, retelling, resisting, and redeeming.[1] By examining each of these four strategies, Black women may unite their corporate suffering with admiration for Mary in a way that blesses spiritual formation.

---

1. Copeland, "Wading Through Many Sorrows," 123–24.

REMEMBERING

Black faith did not originate after chattel slavery. The religions of trafficked and enslaved people often involved a connection to the ancestors. Likewise, we are unable to construct any aspect of womanist theology unless we remember our ancestors whose sufferings and triumphs contribute to the experience that we have today. To create a womanist theology, we must bear in mind all that our Black female ancestors endured: capture, trafficking, whipping, poking, prodding, fondling, raping, demeaning, and child abduction. We must remember the ones who "came through" and have "gone on to glory land."[2] Without this foundation, a womanist theology is nearly impossible to create.

RETELLING

The Black church has a rich tradition of testimony during worship. A member of the congregation may speak out about the way God has blessed them so that all may offer praises of thanksgiving. By retelling the tales of our ancestors, we "recenter" their position relative to the Word; we also draw strength from them by recalling their acts of resistance, lament, and survival.[3] Doing this gives us a playbook we may use when we encounter suffering.

RESISTANCE

A womanist Mariology must be resistant. Throughout history, Black women have called on their guts and guile to resist the systemic oppression they encounter. Whether through "sass," as Copland mentions, or through physical courage and grit, a womanist outlook must originate from a place of resistance to the empire that oppresses them.[4] This resistance also includes rejection of white patriarchal standards of virtue and desirability. In our womanist Mariology, we must pay extra care to resist the cult of true womanhood and its notions of purity and virginity. Copland writes, "Because of the rape, seduction, and concubinage of Black women under

2. Ibid.
3. Ibid., 123.
4. Ibid., 124.

chattel slavery, chastity or virginity begs new meaning."[5] In a womanist Mariology, we resist confining Mary to a narrow identity based solely on her purity or virtue.

REDEMPTION

Finally, the ethos of a womanist Mariology must include space for Black women to seek redemption. Throughout the writings of enslaved women comes a call for Jesus to redeem them through his sacrifice on the cross. While Black women need Jesus' crucifixion as a salvific act, they also receive the gift of Jesus as a divine co-sufferer. In a world that has often tried to strip Black womanhood of humanity, God's decision to become incarnated as Jesus gives Black women a way to view themselves as created in God's image: a human who endured great societal injustice and physical suffering.

These four elements—remembering, retelling, resistance, and redemption—are the four corners in which we can create a worthy space for a womanist Mariology. Just as Mary has been given many titles over the centuries, I have given her titles of my own, rooted in a womanist reverence.

MARY, BLACK AND BEAUTIFUL

We have no way to know what Mary may have looked like; however, a womanist Mary breaks free from the image of the pale "white queen" who has dominated in images presented by the Western church for generations. While the historical Mary would have looked like a Jewish girl from Judea, our womanist Mary is Black and beautiful. She has deep brown skin and clouds of coily hair. This Mary is not ashamed of her Blackness, much like the woman in Song of Solomon, who states, "Do not gaze at me because I am dark, because the sun has gazed on me" (Song 1:6a). *Mary, Black and Beautiful* relishes the way that sun and melanin have darkened her skin. Her beauty exists wholly outside of the white standard of beauty aligned with the cult of true womanhood.

5. Ibid., 111.

MARY, KEEPER OF OUR VINEYARD

> My mother's sons were angry with me; they made me keeper of the
> vineyards,but my own vineyard I have not kept! (Song 1:6b)

A womanist Mary keeps her own vineyard. Black women in history carried
the burden of toiling for white families at the complete expense of their
own. Their youth, energy, time, and nourishment was taken and exploited
by others. Also, Black women have taken on the role of the "strong Black
woman" who is expected to exist as an ever-ready caretaker for both her
oppressors as well as for the Black family. The "strong Black woman" is supposed to bear babies, work long and arduous hours, build up Black men,
and fight for justice for their entire race. Black women often lead move-
ments that cater to the liberation of Black men, not women. What Black
women are not expected to do, however, is care for themselves.

In the Gospel of John, Mary implored her Son Jesus to perform his
first public miracle; changing water into wine at the wedding in Cana.
While Jesus told her that it was "not yet his time," Mary compelled him to
perform this miracle of hospitality, abundance, and luxury. He did not just
make wine; he made fine wine, as the wedding guests commented that the
hosts had saved the good stuff for last. Just as she compelled Jesus to make
a wealth of wine, *Mary, Keeper of Our Vineyard* reminds Black women that
they deserve abundance and luxury, especially that which Jesus provides
through his radical love for the outsider. Many wonder why Mary urged Jesus to perform this miracle before he was ready. *Mary, Keeper of Our Vineyard* asked him to do it so that Black women may take a seat at the banquet
table and partake in the good stuff, enjoying well-deserved hospitality and
rest. Until his return, Black women must tend to our vineyards, as Mary
reminds us to do so.

MARY, KEEPER OF GOOD COMPANY

Tamar, Rahab, Ruth, and Bathsheba: these are the four women who are
mentioned in the genealogy of Jesus given at the beginning of the Gospel of Matthew. Each of these women were outsiders. They also used their
sexual and reproductive acts in subversive ways. Tamar played the prostitute, becoming impregnated by her father-in-law to get what was rightfully
hers. Rahab was a woman who used her sexual desirability to protect an

entire people.[6] Ruth was an ethnic outsider who was unusually close to her mother-in-law, Naomi. The two women devised a plan for Ruth to seduce a man to marry well and provide for their well-being. Then came Bathsheba, who became pregnant in an act of adultery with the beloved King David, who had Bathsheba's husband, Uriah, killed.

Finally, Mary appears in this family tree. Mary, young, inexperienced, and afraid, became pregnant under unusual circumstances like all the others. Mary's taking by the Spirit left her single and pregnant. As a result of the intrusion into her unmarried womb, the Son of Man was born. As a young girl without sexual agency who became pregnant when she did not expect to, Mary is relatable for all of the young Black girls and women who became pregnant without the power of choice, but whose children were their life's blessing. Mary accepted the annunciation, but she did not set out to choose pregnancy for herself. However, when Mary bravely said yes to God, she also said yes to her child, Jesus, who was the biggest blessing there ever was. An imperfect situation created a perfect savior for the world. Like the four women who came before her, Mary is an example of the realities of female sexuality and survival, and the ability to thrive despite those harsh realities.

MARY, MOTHER OF THE MOVEMENT

Mary's son Jesus was a revolutionary. He was a man who was considered subversive and challenged those in power. He was homeless, a drifter, an itinerant preacher, and an activist. In the end, he was executed by the state; Mary had no choice but to watch powerlessly at the cross.

Mary's son, of course, was resurrected and triumphed over his unjust death. However, for the mothers of marginalized individuals killed by police or racialized violence, there is no such happy ending. For these women, who have become the "mothers of the movement" devoted to ending police brutality, Mary acts as a mother in solidarity. Jesus is known as the "first fruits," being raised from the dead and ascending into heaven. For those who have lost their children, the eschatological hope that their bodies will be raised from the dead and greeted in heaven holds great importance. Mary was the first to receive this gift, and she represents the marginalized mothers of the movement whose sons and daughters were misunderstood,

6. See Wil Gafney's sermon "Remixed Gospel of Rahab" for a womanist analysis of this Old Testament text.

reviled and killed. *Mary, Mother of the Movement* empathizes completely in this particular grief.

MARY, MAKER OF SOMETHING WITH NOTHING

When I was a child, my mother used to stretch the last of the orange juice by adding water and a bit of sugar. When my brother and I asked what it was we were drinking, her answer was, "Mommy-made-it, that's what." While my childhood was quite privileged compared to many others, my mother possessed the special ability of Black mothers to make something out of nothing.

Lacking adequate food, clothing, and resources to meet their children's needs, Black mothers are famous for making something out of nothing. An old family friend used to routinely feed her children rice and eggs as a meal because of its low cost. As an adult, one of her sons was surprised that his bride did not know of his favorite comfort dish; he had no idea it wasn't a typical family meal. Likewise, soul food cooking is born out of the ingenuity of Black cooks who took the worst cuts of meat and the wild greens of plants to create soul-satisfying meals.

In the gospel accounts of Mary's pregnancy and Jesus' birth, it seems that she certainly did not have what she needed to ideally care for a baby. In modern terms, she did not have a sterile birthing suite or a department store registry with all of the necessary baby gear. The Son of Man was born in a manger because there was no place for them at the inn (perhaps the innkeeper did not like her kind—a sort of first-century Jim Crow). She wrapped him in bands of cloth; perhaps she did not have fresh swaddling clothes.

As discussed earlier in this chapter, it was Mary's idea to make something out of nothing by asking Jesus to change water to wine. The ability to make something out of nothing is a skill that Jesus kept with him throughout his ministry, stretching fishes and loaves to feed thousands. Sometimes he even had leftovers. *Mary, Maker of Something with Nothing* helps us to remember and retell the stories of our foremothers who knew this skill. Today we give our testimony of the ways that Black mothers have expertly stretched a plate and a dollar to feed their children.

MARY, PERPETUALLY HER OWN

Mary is known throughout much of Christendom as the perpetual virgin. As discussed in previous chapters, this is an impossible standard for Black women (or any women) to emulate. For Black women, whose bodies have been treated as chattel and battlegrounds, perpetual virginity is of no use.

What a womanist Mary is, however, is perpetually her own. Without the interference of male aggression or seduction, this Mary can concentrate on her worth as a highly favored, God-created being. Her self-determination, faith in the Godhead, and personal relationship with Jesus define her, not a sexual partnership or sexual status.

To invoke Sojourner Truth's quote a final time: "Where did your Christ come from? Where did your Christ come from? From God and a woman! Man had nothing to do with him." Mary's miracle is not her perpetual virginity but her ability to allow God to create life within her without the participation of a man. *Mary, Perpetually Her Own* gives an example of the body autonomy that centuries of Black women have not been afforded. She gives women the eschatological hope that when in God's realm their bodies will belong only to themselves and their Creator.

BLACK MADONNA—OUR PROTOTYPE

Powder blue is to the Virgin Mary as sapphire is to the Black Madonna.

Alice Walker tells us that feminism is to lavender as womanism is to purple. When it comes to Mariology, the powder blue that the Mary of images often wears represents the traditional Marian cult. A Black Madonna, however, wears a deep, brilliant, rich sapphire blue.[7]

The Black Madonna is a prototype for Black motherhood. The fullness and complexity of the Black Madonna provide a spiritual inspiration that Black women may appreciate. Finally, the Black Madonna gives us an entirely unique way in which to experience the incarnation of Jesus Christ. The Black Madonna has the rareness, darkness, solidity, and preciousness of a sapphire. May all generations call her blessed.

---

7. The use of the word "sapphire" is not accidental. It reclaims the word used to limit and demean Black women as a stereotype.

BIBLIOGRAPHY

Alvarez, Lizette, and Cara Buckley. "Zimmerman Is Acquitted in Trayvon Martin Killing." *New York Times*, July 13, 2013. http://www.nytimes.com/2013/07/14/us/george-zimmerman-verdict-trayvon-martin.html.

Anderson, Elisha. "Manslaughter Charge Dismissed in Cop's Shooting of Girl." *USA Today*, October 3, 2014. http://www.usatoday.com/story/news/nation/2014/10/03/detroit-girl-killed-police-manslaughter-charge-dropped/16644447.

Awad, Najib. "Elaboration on the First Quest." Class lecture from the course "Looking at Jesus Christ in the Context of the Modern World," Hartford Seminary. February 17, 2016.

Ayoub, Mahmoud. *Redemptive Suffering in Islām: A Study of the Devotional Aspects of 'Āshūrā' in Twelver Shī'ism*. The Hague: Mouton, 1978.

Balserak, Jon, and Beth Kreitzer. "Reforming Mary: Changing Images of the Virgin Mary in Lutheran Sermons of the Sixteenth Century." *Sixteenth Century Journal* 36.4 (2005) 1192. doi:10.2307/20477655.

Beauvoir, Simone de. *The Second Sex*. New York: Vintage, 2011.

Bhabha, Homi. "Of Mimicry and Man: The Ambivalence of Colonial Discourse." *October* 28 (1984) 125. doi: 10.2307/778467.

Borg, Marcus J., and N. T. Wright. *The Meaning of Jesus: Two Visions*. San Francisco: HarperSanFrancisco, 1999.

Buduson, Sarah. "CMSD Resource Officer Under Investigation after NewsChannel 5 Asks About His Tamir Rice Comments." News 5 Cleveland, January 4, 2016. http://www.newsnet5.com/news/local-news/investigations/cmsd-resource-officer-under-investigation-after-newschannel-5-asks-about-his-tamir-rice-comments.

Caswall, Edward. *Lyra Catholica: Containing All the Breviary and Missal Hymns with Others from Various Sources*. London: Burns and Oates, 1884.

Chappell, Bill. "Texas Pool Party Update: Teens and Residents Speak Out." *The Two-Way*, NPR, June 8, 2015. http://www.npr.org/sections/thetwo-way/2015/06/08/412889290/texas-pool-party-update-teens-and-residents-speak-out.

Clooney, Francis X. "Mary in the Quran." *America*, December 18, 2015. http://www.americamagazine.org/content/all-things/maryam-mother-jesus-quran.

Copeland, M. Shawn. "Wading Through Many Sorrows." In *A Troubling in My Soul: Womanist Perspectives on Evil and Suffering*, edited by Emilie M. Townes, 109–29. Maryknoll, NY: Orbis, 1993.

Crisp, Oliver D. "On the 'Fittingness' of the Virgin Birth." *Heythrop Journal* 49.2 (2008) 197–221. doi:10.1111/j.1468-2265.2007.00336.x.

Daly, Mary. *Beyond God the Father: Toward a Philosophy of Women's Liberation.* Boston: Beacon, 1973.

————. *The Church and the Second Sex.* New York: Harper & Row, 1975.

Davary, Bahar. "Mary in Islam: No Man Could Have Been Like This Woman." *New Theology Review* 23.3 (August 2010) 26-34. http://newtheologyreview.org/index.php/ntr/article/viewFile/849/1036.

Davis, Deirdre. "The Harm That Has No Name: Street Harassment, Embodiment, and African American Women." *UCLA Women's Law Journal* 4.2 (1994) 133-78. http://escholarship.org/uc/item/83b9f21g.

Demby, Gene. "The Truth Behind the Lies of the Original 'Welfare Queen.'" *Codeswitch,* NPR, December 20, 2013. http://www.npr.org/sections/codeswitch/2013/12/20/255819681/the-truth-behind-the-lies-of-the-original-welfare-queen.

DeSilva, David Arthur. *The Hope of Glory: Honor Discourse and New Testament Interpretation.* Collegeville, MN: Liturgical, 1999.

Elizabeth (1765?-1866). *Elizabeth, a Colored Minister of the Gospel Born in Slavery.* Chapel Hill: Academic Affairs Library, University of North Carolina at Chapel Hill, 1999. http://docsouth.unc.edu/neh/eliza2/eliza2.html. Originally published, Philadelphia: Tract Association of Friends, 1889.

Elizondo, Virgilio. "Mary in the Struggles of the Poor." *New Catholic World* 229.1374 (November/December 1986) 244-47.

Epiphanius. *The Panarion of Epiphanius of Salamis.* Translated by Frank Williams. 2nd ed., revised and expanded. Leiden: Brill, 2009.

Esposito, John L. *What Everyone Needs to Know about Islam.* Oxford: Oxford University Press, 2002.

Feldstein, Ruth. "I Wanted the Whole World to See." In *Not June Cleaver: Women and Gender in Postwar America, 1945-1960,* edited by Joanne Meyerowitz, 263-303. Philadelphia: Temple University Press, 1994.

Ferrise, Adam. "Tamir Rice's Sister: Cleveland Police Officer 'Attacked Me.'" *Cleveland.com,* December 14, 2014. http://www.cleveland.com/metro/index.ssf/2014/12/tamir_rices_sister_cleveland_p.html.

Fitzmyer, Joseph A. *The Gospel According to Luke.* Garden City, NY: Doubleday, 1981.

Ford, Dana, and Chelsea J. Carter. "Justice System 'Didn't Work for Us,' Trayvon Martin's Father Says." *CNN,* July 18, 2013. http://cnn.com/2013/07/18/ustice/trayvon-martin-parents/.

Gafney, Wil. "Remixed Gospel of Rahab: Who Are You Calling a Whore?" October 2014. http://www.wilgafney.com/tag/rahab/.

Golston, Hilary. "Attorney: Mother of Tamir Rice Wept So Much She Couldn't Speak." WKYC, December 29, 2015. http://www.wkyc.com/news/local/cleveland/attorney-mother-of-tamir-rice-wept-so-much-she-couldnt-speak/15131278.

Goodacre, Mark. "Scripturalization in Mark's Crucifixion Narrative." In *The Trial and Death of Jesus: Essays on the Passion Narrative in Mark,* edited by Geert Van Oyen and Tom Shepherd, 33-47. Leuven: Peeters, 2006:

"Grandmother's Fingerprints, DNA Not Found on Officer Weekley's Submachine Gun." WXYZ, October 2, 2014. https://web.archive.org/web/20160411161132/http://www.wxyz.com/news/grandmothers-fingerprints-dna-not-found-on-officer-weekleys-submachine-gun.

Gray, Mary C. "Reclaiming Mary: A Task for Feminist Theology." *Way* 29 (1989) 334-40.

Green, Laura. "Stereotypes: Negative Racial Stereotypes and Their Effect on Attitudes Toward African-Americans." *Perspectives on Multiculturalism and Cultural Diversity.* 11.1 (Winter 1998–99). http://www.ferris.edu/jimcrow/links/VCU.htm.

Gutherie, Doug, and Hunter, George. "Slain Girl's Family Alleges Police Cover-Up." *The Detroit News,* May 19, 2010. http://www.detnews.com/article/20100519/ METRO01/5190376/1409/metro/Slain-girl-s-family-alleges-police-cover-up.

Gutiérrez, Gustavo. *A Theology of Liberation: History, Politics, and Salvation.* Maryknoll, NY: Orbis, 1973.

Haddad, G. F. "A Critical Reading of Martin Lings' *Muhammad: His Life Based on the Earliest Sources.*" Foreword to the first Swedish translation. *at-Tahawi,* May 30, 2015. https://attahawi.com/2015/05/30/a-critical-reading-of-martin-lings-muhammad-his-life-based-on-the-earliest-sources/.

Hallam, Jennifer. "The Slave Experience: Family." *Slavery and the Making of America,* PBS, 2004. http://www.pbs.org/wnet/slavery/experience/family/history.html.

———. "The Slave Experience: Men, Women, and Gender." *Slavery and the Making of America,* PBS, 2004. http://www.pbs.org/wnet/slavery/experience/gender/history. html.

Harris, Stephen. *The New Testament: A Student's Introduction.* 8th ed. New York: McGraw Hill Education, 2015.

Hartnett, Daniel. "Remembering the Poor: An Interview with Gustavo Gutiérrez." *America,* February 3, 2013. http://www.americamagazine.org/issue/420/article/ remembering-the-poor-interview-gustavo-gutirrez.

Hengel, Martin. *Crucifixion in the Ancient World and the Folly of the Message of the Cross.* Philadelphia: Fortress, 1977.

hooks, bell. *Black Looks: Race and Representation.* Boston: South End, 1992.

Hopkins, Dwight N., and Linda E. Thomas. *Walk Together Children: Black and Womanist Theologies, Church and Theological Education.* Eugene, OR: Cascade, 2010.

Ibn Hishām, 'Abd al-Malik, and Muhammad Ibn Isḥāk. *The Life of Muhammad: A Translation of Ishāq's Sīrat Rasūl Allāh.* London: Oxford University Press, 1955.

Izadi, Elahe, and Holley, Peter. "Video Shows Cleveland Officer Shooting 12-Year-Old Tamir Rice within Seconds." *Washington Post,* November 26, 2014. https://www. washingtonpost.com/news/post-nation/wp/2014/11/26/officials-release-video-names-in-fatal-police-shooting-of-12-year-old-cleveland-boy/.

Jacobs, Harriet A. *Incidents in the Life of a Slave Girl: Written by Herself.* Edited by Lydia Maria Child. Cambridge, MA: Harvard University Press, 1987.

Jewell, K. Sue. *From Mammy to Miss America and Beyond: Cultural Images and the Shaping of US Social Policy.* London: Routledge, 1993.

Johnson, Elizabeth A. *Truly Our Sister: A Theology of Mary in the Communion of Saints.* New York: Continuum, 2013.

Jones, Jacqueline. *Labor of Love, Labor of Sorrow: Black Women, Work, and the Family, from Slavery to the Present.* New York: Basic Books, 2010.

Junior, Nyasha. *An Introduction to Womanist Biblical Interpretation.* Louisville: Westminster John Knox, 2015.

Kähler, Martin. *The So-Called Historical Jesus and the Historic, Biblical Christ.* Minneapolis: Ausburg Fortress, 1964.

Kierkegaard, Søren. *Parables of Kierkegaard.* Edited by Thomas C. Oden. Princeton, NJ: Princeton University Press, 1978.

Knox v. Hetrick. 2009-Ohio-1359.

Larimer, Sarah. "Disgraced Ex-Officer Daniel Holtzclaw to Be Sentenced after Sex Crimes." *Washington Post*, January 22, 2016. https://www.washingtonpost.com/news/post-nation/wp/2016/01/21/disgraced-ex-officer-daniel-holtzclaw-to-be-sentenced-after-sex-crimes-conviction/?utm_term=.4b6379ce2034.

Lings, Martin. *Muhammad: His Life Based on the Earliest Sources*. New York: Inner Traditions, 1983.

Leith, Mary Joan Winn. "The Virgin Mary and the Prophet Muhammad." *Bible History Daily*, November 1, 2016. http://www.biblicalarchaeology.org/daily/biblical-topics/bible-interpretation/the-virgin-mary-and-the-prophet-muhammad/.

Lenski Gerhard. *Power and Privilege: A Theory of Social Stratification*. New York: McGraw Hill, 1996.

Luther, Martin. *The Annotated Luther*. Vol. 4, *Pastoral Writings*. Edited by Mary Jane Haemig. Minneapolis: Fortress, 2016.

Malbon, Elizabeth Struthers. "Gospel of Mark." In *Women's Bible Commentary*, edited by Carol A. Newsom, Sharon H. Ringe, and Jacqueline E. Lapsley. 3rd ed. Louisville: Westminster John Knox, 2012.

Malloy, Daniel. "Julian Bond Tells of Family's Slave History at March on Washington." *Atlanta Journal Constitution*, August 28, 2013. http://www.ajc.com/news/national-govt—politics/julian-bond-tells-family-slave-history-march-washington/DBfo3rkn5qlAIog2zokODK/.

Margerie, Bertrand de. "Mary in Latin American Liberation Theologies." *Marian Studies* 38.1 (1987) 47–62. http://ecommons.udayton.edu/marian_studies/vol38/iss1/.

"Mary Is with Us in Our Struggles, Pope Francis Teaches." Catholic News Agency, August 15, 2013. http://www.catholicnewsagency.com/news/mary-is-with-us-in-our-struggles-pope-francis-teaches/.

Matthews, Aisha. "Raping the Jezebel Hypocrisy, Stereotyping and Sexual Identity in Harriet Jacobs' Incidents in the Life of a Slavegirl." *International Journal of English Language, Literature, and Humanities* 4.5 (May 2016). doi:10.18411/d-2016-154.

Merchant, Nomaan, and Talley, Tim. "Witness Credibility a Focus in Ex-Officer's Sex Abuse Trial." *U.S. News & World Report*, December 2, 2015. http://www.usnews.com/news/us/articles/2015/12/02/witness-credibility-a-focus-in-ex-officers-sex-abuse-trial.

Mintz, Steven. "Childhood and Transatlantic Slavery." *Children and Youth in History*, Item 57. Center for History and New Media, George Mason University. https://chnm.gmu.edu/cyh/case-studies/57.

Miranda, Carolina A. "Q&A Kara Walker on the Bit of Sugar Sphinx She Saved, Video She's Making." *Los Angeles Times*, October 13, 2014. http://www.latimes.com/entertainment/arts/miranda/la-et-cam-kara-walker-on-her-sugar-sphinx-the-piece-she-saved-video-shes-making-20141013-column.html.

"More Slavery at the South." *Documenting the American South*. University Library, University of North Carolina at Chapel Hill, 2004. http://docsouth.unc.edu/fpn/negnurse/negnurse.html.

Morry, Matthew. "The Magnificat: Reflections." *Marian Studies* 38.1 (1987) 63–77.

"Mosque Dedicated to Virgin Mary Opens in Tartous." *Daily Star* (Lebanon), June 8, 2015. http://www.dailystar.com.lb/News/Middle-East/2015/Jun-08/301021-mosque-dedicated-to-virgin-mary-opens-in-tartous.ashx.

"The Murder of Emmett Till: People and Events – Mamie Till Mobley." PBS. http://www.pbs.org/wgbh/amex/till/peopleevents/p_parents.html.

"The Murder of Emmett Till: Timeline." PBS. http://www.pbs.org/wgbh/amex/till/timeline/timeline2.html.

Nasr, Seyyed Hossein, translator and editor. *The Study Quran: A New Translation and Commentary.* New York: HarperOne, 2015.

Neyrey, Jerome. "Despising the Shame of the Cross: Honor and Shame in the Johannine Passion Narrative." N.d. https://www3.nd.edu/~jneyrey1/shame.html.

Nolan, Mary Catherine. "The Magnificat, Canticle of a Liberated People: A Hermeneutical Study of Luke 1:46–55 Investigating the World Behind the Text by Exegesis; the World in Front of the Text by Interpretive Inquiry." PhD diss., Dayton University, 1995.

Nowak, Vikki. "Forest Hill Church Holds Conversations on Race." *Heights Observer,* November 1, 2011. http://heightsobserver.org/read/2011/11/01/forest-hill-church-holds-coversations-on-race.

Parkhurst, Jessie W. "The Role of the Black Mammy in the Plantation Household." *Journal of Negro History* 23.3 (1938) 349–69. doi:10.2307/2714687.

Parkinson, Justin. "The Significance of Sarah Baartman." *BBCNews Magazine,* January 7, 2016. http://www.bbc.com/news/magazine-35240987.

Parlett, Martin A. *Demonizing a President: The "Foreignization" of Barack Obama.* Santa Barbara, CA: Praeger, 2014.

Paul VI, Pope. *Lumen Gentium.* November 21, 1964. http://www.vatican.va/archive/hist_councils/ii_vatican_council/documents/vat-ii_const_19641121_lumen-gentium_en.html.

Pelikan, Jaroslav. *Mary Through the Centuries: Her Place in the History of Culture.* New Haven, CT: Yale University Press, 1996.

Pius IX, Pope. *Ineffabilis Deus.* December 8, 1854. http://www.papalencyclicals.net/Pius09/p9ineff.htm.

Pius XII, Pope. *Ad Caeli Reginam.* October 11, 1954. http://www.papalencyclicals.net/Pius12/P12CAELI.HTM.

———. *Munificentissimus Deus.* November 1, 1950. http://w2.vatican.va/content/pius-xii/en/apost_constitutions/documents/hf_p-xii_apc_19501101_munificentissimus-deus.html.

———. *Sacra Virginitas.* March 25, 1954. http://w2.vatican.va/content/pius-xii/en/encyclicals/documents/hf_p-xii_enc_25031954_sacra-virginitas.html.

"Prosecutor: No Third Trial for Officer in Death of Aiyana Stanley-Jones." WJBK, Fox 2 Detroit, January 28, 2015. http://www.fox2detroit.com/news/183816-story.

Ratzinger, Joseph. "Thoughts on the Place of Marian Doctrine and Piety in Faith and Theology as a Whole." *Communio International Catholic Review* 30.1 (Spring 2003) 147–60.

Reid, Joy-Ann. "Lawyer for Tamir Rice's Mother Blasts Prosecutor's Remarks." *MSNBC,* November 7, 2015. http://www.msnbc.com/msnbc/lawyer-tamir-rices-mother-blasts-prosecutors-remarks.

Ruether, Rosemary Radford. *Sexism and God-Talk: Toward a Feminist Theology.* Boston: Beacon, 1983.

Schaeffer, Jim. "Detroit Police Outline Final Moments of Aiyana's Life." Detroit Free Press, May 19, 2010. https://web.archive.org/web/20100522064638/http://www.freep.com/article/20100519/NEWS01/5190356/0/BUSINESS06.

Schüssler Fiorenza, Elisabeth. *Jesus: Miriam's Child, Sophia's Prophet: Critical Issues in Feminist Christology.* 2nd ed. New York: Bloomsbury T. & T. Clark, 2015.

"Second Mistrial Declared in Fatal Shooting of Aiyana Stanley-Jones by Detroit Police Officer Joseph Weekley." CBS News, October 10, 2014. http://www.cbsnews.com/news/second-mistrial-in-detroit-cops-fata-shooting-of-girl-7/.

Smith, J. I., and Y. Y. Haddad. "The Virgin Mary in Islamic Tradition and Commentary." The Muslim World 79 (1989) 161–87. doi:10.1111/j.1478-1913.198"9.tb02846.x.

Stowasser, Barbara Freyer. Women in the Qur'an, Traditions, and Interpretation. New York: Oxford University Press, 1994.

Strauss, David Friedrich. The Life of Jesus, Critically Examined. Philadelphia: Fortress, 1973.

Thompson, Nato. "Curatorial Statement." Creative Time Presents Kara Walker. Nd. http://creativetime.org/projects/karawalker/curatorial-statement/.

Thurman, Howard. Jesus and the Disinherited. Boston, MA: Beacon, 1996.

Truth, Sojourner. Narrative of Sojourner Truth: with "Book of Life" and "A Memorial Chapter". New York: Barnes & Noble Classics, 2005.

USCCB (United States Conference of Catholic Bishops. Catechism of the Catholic Church. 2nd ed. English translation. Washington, DC: USCCB, 1994. http://ccc.usccb.org/flipbooks/catechism/index.html.

"The Virgin Mary in Islamic-Christian Dialogue." Vidimus Dominum, March 20, 2014. http://vd.pcn.net/en/index.php?option=com_content&view=article&id=1425:the-virgin-mary-in-islamic-christian-dialogue&catid=22:interreligious-dialog&Itemid=9.

"Vittorio Messori and 'The Mary Hypothesis.'" ZENIT, English ed., November 25, 2005. https://zenit.org/articles/vittorio-messori-and-the-mary-hypothesis/.

West, Carolyn M. "Mammy, Sapphire, and Jezebel: Historical Images of Black Women and Their Implications for Psychotherapy." Psychotherapy 32.3 (1995) 458–66. doi:10.1037/0033-3204.32.3.458.

Williams, Patricia. "Spirit-Murdering the Messenger: The Discourse of Fingerpointing as the Law's Response to Racism." University of Miami's Law Review 42.127 (1987) 127–57. http://repository.law.miami.edu/umlr/vol42/iss1/8/.

Winfrey Harris, Tamara. The Sisters Are Alright: Changing the Broken Narrative of Black Women in America. Oakland: Berrett-Koehler, 2015.

INDEX OF AUTHORS

INDEX OF ANCIENT DOCUMENTS

CPSIA information can be obtained
at www.ICGtesting.com
Printed in the USA
BVOW09*0521051017
496713BV00004B/170/P